PREPARING STUDENTS TO RAISE ACHIEVEMENT SCORES

Grades 5–6

by Darriel Ledbetter and
Leland Graham

Incentive Publications, Inc.
Nashville, Tennessee

The authors gratefully acknowledge
the assistance and suggestions of the following persons:

Virginia Brickman, Stan Carey, Brenda Colburn, Harriett Cook,
Shirley Copeland, Dan Gasparrini and Instructional Informatics, Inc.,
Chris Higgins, Jeremy Hinds, Sue Kennedy, Robert Kingsbury,
Frankie Long, Isabelle McCoy, Beverly Moody, Jennifer Moore,
Melanie Moore, Umar Sayed, Laura Sharp, Pat Slaton,
Clare Vickers, and Nancy Zwald.

Illustrated by Kathleen Bullock
Cover by Marta Drayton and Joe Shibley

ISBN 0-86530-333-9

PRINTED IN THE UNITED STATES OF AMERICA

Table of Contents

INTRODUCTION

It has become increasingly important that children be trained to improve the skills that allow them to succeed when taking standardized tests. National average achievement standards are being developed for all ages and for all academic areas. The best classes, schools, and futures will belong to those students who develop the best test-taking skills.

There are many different types of achievement tests. Students should learn a variety of strategies and skills so that their true knowledge is reflected in all achievement scores. Test-taking skills in this book include those in the following areas:

reading comprehension;

vocabulary and spelling;

math concepts and computations;

language mechanics;

interpreting maps, charts, and diagrams; and

use of the library.

Parents and teachers who help students learn to make use of the test-taking strategies and skills in this book will invariably see students' achievement scores improve. An improvement in achievement scores means positive reinforcement of a student's self-confidence, resulting in improved performance in all areas of academic work.

CHAPTER ONE:

MASTERING STUDY TECHNIQUES AND TEST-TAKING SKILLS

In this chapter you will find the basic techniques that will help you study more effectively and improve your test scores. In order to make the best use of these skills, follow these helpful study hints:

- **Find a proper study area in which to work.**
  The best place would be a quiet, well-lighted study area away from family interruptions, distractions, and conversations.

- **Designate a regular study time or period.**
  Set aside time each day to study. During this designated time, all other activities should cease: no phone calls, no television, no friends' visits, and no interruptions from parents or other family members.

- **Keep a daily, weekly, or monthly planner.**
  Keeping a planner (see following pages) is a good way to keep track of all of your assignments, upcoming tests, after-school activities, family outings, and household chores. The left column of the daily planner is for listing assignments for various periods. The right column will help you plan your day as well as schedule appointments and events. Make a copy of the daily assignment planner and list your current subjects in order. Then make enough copies of this master planning page to serve your needs.

- **Obtain all the proper materials for your study area.**
  Be sure to have all the proper school supplies that you need in order to study. Your study area should include: pencils, colored pencils, pens, pencil sharpener, erasers, three-hole lined paper, three-ring binder, ruler, highlighter, paper clips, glue stick, index cards, student planner (daily, weekly, or monthly), dictionary, and thesaurus. If you have a home computer, it should be in your study area.

MONTH OF

SUNDAY	MONDAY	TUESDAY	WEDNESDAY	THURSDAY	FRIDAY	SATURDAY

DAILY ASSIGNMENT PLANNER

ASSIGNMENTS   DATE _____

FIRST PERIOD _____

SECOND PERIOD_____

THIRD PERIOD _____

FOURTH PERIOD _____

FIFTH PERIOD _____

SIXTH PERIOD _____

8:00 A.M.

9:00 A.M.

10:00 A.M.

11:00 A.M.

12:00 P.M.

1:00 P.M.

2:00 P.M.

3:00 P.M.

4:00 P.M.

5:00 P.M.

6:00 P.M.

7:00 P.M.

MASTERING STUDY TECHNIQUES AND TEST-TAKING SKILLS

Taking good notes is one of the most useful study skills you will learn. You may think note taking is just for high school or college students, but this is a study skill you should develop as early as fifth or sixth grade. If you become a good note taker, you will do better on tests and written reports.

NOTEWORTHY TIPS . . .

- Prepare your note-taking materials before you go to class (i.e., pencils should already be sharpened).

- Pay close attention to your teacher and concentrate on what he or she is saying.

- Jot down important facts and ideas.

- Use key words, phrases, clauses, or simple sentences to record the information. In other words, don't try to write down the information word for word. Instead, listen to get the main ideas.

- Though you are not taking notes word for word, try to jot down any details, dates, and examples that seem to be the type of information that is often asked on quizzes and tests.

- Whenever possible, use abbreviations and symbols (i.e., January = Jan.; Sunday = Sun.; Alabama = AL; foot = ft.; percent = %).

- Begin to develop your own speed-writing or shorthand system. Much time can be saved by using symbols instead of whole words when you are taking notes (for example: ntbk = notebook; rpt = report; prjct = project; ques = question; dir = directions).

- Learn to ask questions when you do not understand what your teacher or parent means.

- Reread your notes before leaving class to clarify any confusion you may have.

PRACTICE TAKING NOTES

ACTIVITY: Your parent or teacher will read the following paragraphs aloud to you. On a sheet of notebook paper, take notes on the paragraphs using speed-writing symbols, phrases, or clauses. When completed, read your notes aloud to your parent or teacher.

> Kites, named after the graceful kite bird, originated in China over 3000 years ago. Brightly painted kites were used to signal soldiers, scare birds away from crops, catch fish, and frighten bandits from houses. Today people enjoy flying many types of kites as a recreational activity.
>
> From *Pineapples, Penguins, & Pagodas,* Incentive Publications. Used by permission

> Miami, Florida, has long enjoyed a reputation as a romantic city. Each year, thousands of people from all over the world flock to Miami beaches for holiday relaxation and fun. But Miami, as does any large city, also has its sinister side. It has crime, violence, and racial unrest—all the tensions of a world-class population center.
>
> From *Composition & Creative Writing,* Incentive Publications. Used by permission.

> Antarctica, the coolest place on earth, is the fifth largest continent. This ice-covered area completely encircles the South Pole. The continent is surrounded by the Pacific, Atlantic, and Indian Oceans.
>
> Plant fossils have been found in Antarctica, indicating that a warm climate once existed on the continent. Today, however, only a few plants and insects can survive Antarctica's frozen interior. Penguins, whales, krill, birds, and fish live in the surrounding waters.
>
> People do not live on this continent permanently. Scientific research stations are located on Antarctica. All supplies and food must be delivered during the summer months. The summer season is between November and January. Summer temperatures reach 50 degrees Fahrenheit on the northern islands. During the winter season, May to June, the continent is dark with extremely cold weather and dangerous blizzards.
>
> From *Pineapples, Penguins, & Pagodas,* Incentive Publications. Used by permission.

Now that you have practiced taking notes, the next step is to **read** your notes aloud. You and a classmate should read your notes aloud to each other, or read them to a family member. Also, please keep in mind that notes written quickly in class can sometimes be difficult to read and understand. In these cases, while the information is still fresh in your mind, **rewrite** your notes so that you can understand what you have written. You can strengthen or **reinforce** your notes by adding important information from your textbook. Then use a highlighter to **spotlight** important facts, dates, and names in your notes.

In order to remember names, dates, facts, and other information from your notes, develop your own mnemonic devices. A memory device, often written in the right-hand margin, can be a word, phrase, or even a picture. Whatever device you create will help you recall the information while reviewing or taking a test.

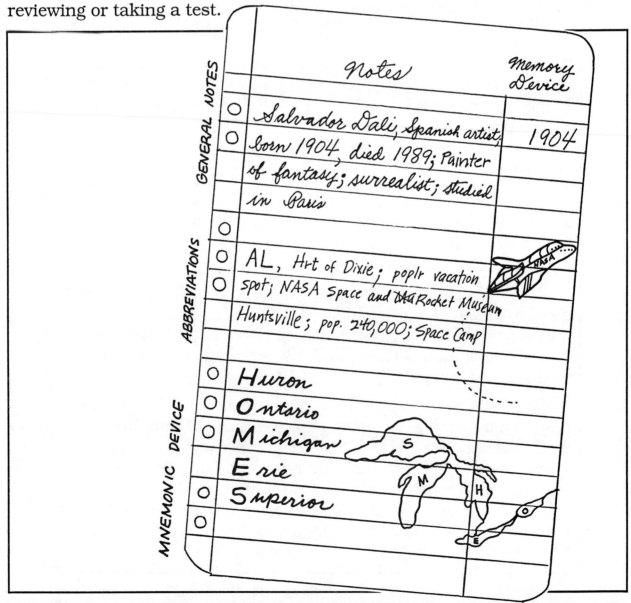

Studying for a test involves many skills. If you have completed all of your classroom and homework assignments, listened carefully, and taken thorough notes, you should be ready for your test review time. The more you study for your test, the more confidence you will naturally have. Here are some **helpful hints** in the final preparation for taking any test:

- **Do not** spend precious time studying information you already know.

- If possible, create your own flash cards (index cards with questions written on one side and answers written on the other side). These cards are useful for learning the most difficult concepts.

- Review your class notes and homework assignments as needed. If necessary, use your mnemonic devices for an additional review. Again, flash cards may be helpful if you are having difficulty remembering the information.

- Finally, study the information you took from your textbook to reinforce your notes. Follow the same procedures as mentioned in your class notes.

How to successfully take tests: The test papers are handed out and the teacher has announced: "Begin!" What should you do next? Take a few minutes or so to . . .

- **Read all of the directions carefully.** (Students often miss test questions because they do not read or understand the directions.)

- **Pay attention to the directions at the bottom of the page.** Sometimes you are instructed to **GO ON** to the next page and other times to **STOP!**

- **Skim the entire test as quickly as possible.**

- **Use your "memory devices."** If necessary, jot down a word or picture on the back of a page in order to jog your memory later.

- **Do not spend too much time on one problem or question.** Mark the troublesome question, move on, and if you have time, go back to it.

- **If you finish your test early,** and if it is permitted, go back and check your work on any "unsure" or marked question(s).

- **Remember, first instincts are generally correct.** Do not make the mistake of second-guessing yourself.

- **Be sure to erase your original answer completely** if you need to change an answer.

- **The best advice:** Make sure you are rested and alert on the day of testing.

CHAPTER TWO:

IMPROVING VOCABULARY SKILLS

In the first chapter, you learned various study techniques and test-taking skills, which are essential to success in taking the Achievement Test. The purpose of this chapter is to improve your vocabulary skills by looking at various strategies to help you understand word usage. These strategies include: sound, structure, context clues, and a dictionary. With a greater understanding of words and how they are used, your vocabulary achievement scores will naturally improve.

ACTIVITY: For each question below, decide which one of the four answers is closest in meaning to the word in bold type above it. Fill in the bubble for the word that is closest in meaning.

 *Think about the meaning of the word (not its part of speech) in **bold type** before you select an answer.*

1. The **proficient** secretary worked hard.

   ○ competent
   ○ lengthy
   ○ favorable
   ○ interesting

2. What an ugly **rumor**!

   ○ well-stated
   ○ gossip
   ○ funny
   ○ solution

3. The full moon was **luminous**.

   ○ glowing
   ○ healthy
   ○ fascinating
   ○ frightening

4. She laid a careful **scheme**.

   ○ scent
   ○ report
   ○ plan
   ○ project

STOP

WORDS AND THEIR MEANINGS

ACTIVITY: For each question, decide which of the four answers has most nearly the same meaning as the word in bold type above it. Circle the correct answer.

1. **Operate** the machinery
   A repair
   B rent
   C work
   D behind

2. The **ruthless** king
   A cruel
   B sad
   C joyful
   D unshaven

3. To hope or to **despair**
   A succeed
   B wish
   C plan
   D give up

4. The **negligent** cashier
   A courteous
   B neglectful
   C eager
   D trustworthy

5. To be **humble**
   A modest
   B disrespectful
   C punctual
   D foolish

6. In a **remorseful** mood
   A repulsive
   B doubtful
   C regretful
   D curious

7. His **reluctance** to leave
   A determination
   B eagerness
   C desire
   D unwillingness

8. **Deplete** your allowance
   A increase
   B use up
   C raise
   D hand over

9. A lifesaving **procedure**
   A machine
   B vaccine
   C method
   D invention

10. During the **launch**
    A beginning
    B landing
    C lecture
    D ceremony

11. The **ambiguous** meaning
   A   single
   B   written
   C   shocking
   D   unclear

12. Quite **stimulating**
   A   arousing
   B   annoying
   C   deceiving
   D   hidden

13. Occasionally **hesitant**
   A   late
   B   willing
   C   undecided
   D   aggressive

14. A funny **anecdote**
   A   song
   B   poem
   C   story
   D   author

15. The **obsolete** computer
   A   outdated
   B   self-instructed
   C   influential
   D   uninteresting

16. Such a **blatant** remark
   A   wise
   B   fine
   C   skillful
   D   loudmouthed

17. **Significant** diagnosis
   A   simple
   B   important
   C   unnecessary
   D   sudden

18. To **conclude**
   A   begin
   B   conduct
   C   terminate
   D   agree

19. **Beneath** the clouds
   A   beyond
   B   under
   C   in
   D   above

20. To **dissipate**
   A   scatter
   B   continue
   C   withhold
   D   rain

I'm hesitant to tell this stimulating, but ambiguous, anecodote.

STOP

WORDS AND THEIR MEANINGS

ACTIVITY: Choose the word
that means the **same** as
(or is a synonym for)
the word in **bold** type.

1. A **thorough** job
   ① thought
   ② complete
   ③ fair
   ④ incomplete

2. The **vacant** lot
   ① occupied
   ② overgrown
   ③ empty
   ④ noisy

3. An **essential** part
   ① optional
   ② unnecessary
   ③ healthy
   ④ necessary

4. **devoid** of furniture
   ① empty
   ② mess
   ③ full
   ④ sale

5. **Liberty** for everyone
   ① slavery
   ② freedom
   ③ justice
   ④ dependence

WORDS AND THEIR MEANINGS

ACTIVITY: Choose the word
that means the **opposite** of
(or is an antonym for)
the word in **bold** type.

6. A **marvelous** idea
   ① strange
   ② horrible
   ③ splendid
   ④ funny

7. A weekend of **tranquility**
   ① excitement
   ② company
   ③ peace
   ④ calm

8. The **oblivious** jury
   ① considerate
   ② aware
   ③ intense
   ④ unmindful

9. To **prevaricate** frequently
   ① lie
   ② cheat
   ③ speak truthfully
   ④ fight

10. To **execute** the order
    ① administer
    ② change
    ③ destroy
    ④ ignore

STOP

WORDS AND THEIR MEANINGS

ACTIVITY: Of the words that **sound alike** (or are homonyms), circle the one that best completes the meaning in the sentence. If there are two blanks in a sentence, write the correct one in its corresponding blank.

1. John saw a _____ in the pasture with a cow.   **horse hoarse**

2. He _____ annoy everyone in his class.   **can't cant**

3. If they are going to succeed, they must
do _____ work.   **they're their there**

4. The teacher found his new pen, _____.   **two to too**

5. _____ see you on the third row and fourth seat.   **I'll Aisle**

6. It was a major _____ for the injured runner.   **feet feat**

7. Even though he is a man, sometimes he will
_____ in the morning.   **groan grown**

8. Two of the dog's _____ were broken, and
the old man took time to _____ and help.   **pause paws**

9. _____ about time to begin planting the new flower bed.   **Its It's**

10. Although my doctor has many _____ ,
he always remains calm and full of _____.   **patience patients**

11. The _____ stated their _____ ,
or rules, on the first day of school.   **principles principals**

12. It _____ that you forgot to sew these
two _____.   **seams seems**

13. If the sports event is next _____ , I will be
too _____ to attend.   **weak week**

14. We stayed in the deluxe hotel _____ where
guests are given _____ chocolates upon arrival.   **sweet suite**

15. If your _____ is over 142 pounds, you will
have to _____ until tomorrow to wrestle.   **wait weight**

16. Do you know how much the train _____ is
to the state _____ in Knoxville?   **fair fare**

STOP

ORIGIN OF WORDS

ACTIVITY: Read the meaning given for each word. Decide which present-day word comes from the original word. Circle your answer.

1. Which word may have come from the German word **schichten,** meaning *arranging in order*?

   A. ship   B. sail   C. shift   D. move

2. Which word probably came from the Latin word **honorarius,** relating to *honor*?

   A. position   B. recognition   C. token   D. honorary

3. Which word probably came from the Latin word **humanus,** meaning *of a man*?

   A. human   B. humus   C. humorous   D. humor

4. Which word may have come from the Latin word **falsus,** meaning *deceptive*?

   A. flaw   B. flare   C. false   D. falcon

5. Which word may have come from the Old English word **drifan,** meaning *drive*?

   A. different   B. impulse   C. carry   D. drift

STOP

CHOOSING THE CORRECT WORD

ACTIVITY: Read the paragraphs. Decide which of the words from each numbered list completes the meaning in the corresponding blank. Circle the letter next to the chosen word.

During the Middle Ages, Christianity became a force that brought most of Europe together. ____(1)____ became Christians, and missionaries began to travel all over the world spreading the doctrine of faith. Eventually the church became a very powerful force in government, establishing a court system for offenders and a tax system to help run the government.

As Christianity flourished, centers of spiritual learning were founded and called ____(2)____. The men who ran the monasteries were called monks. They devoted their whole lives to serving God, giving up worldly ____(3)____ and pleasures. Furthermore, the monks were generally the only people who could read and write, usually in Latin. Because of these skills, they were very important in the ____(4)____ of valuable writings and the founding of schools.

1. A. Monks
   B. Ministers
   C. Women
   D. Barbarians

2. A. monasteries
   B. government
   C. crusades
   D. missionaries

3. A. control
   B. learning
   C. possessions
   D. food

4. A. reading
   B. preservation
   C. destruction
   D. historic

STOP

LEARNING VOCABULARY WORDS

ACTIVITY: Choose the word from the list that best completes the meaning of each sentence. Fill in the blank with the letter representing that word.

1. The dinosaurs belonged to a prehistoric _____.

2. Levente is a _____ young man in his ironed shirt, tie, and trousers.

3. Do the words at the end of the line _____?

4. Exercise _____ as you take the detour.

5. It seems the block party every July has become an _____ event.

6. I can always count on my mom for good _____.

7. The _____ stepped out of the plane unhurt.

8. Mikc's old mare looks _____ and sick.

9. When one visits the Forum in Rome, Italy, the 2,000 year-old _____ city comes to life.

10. Studying vocabulary will _____ one to improve his achievement scores.

11. The teacher asked us to describe the _____ because the sun and its rays were so beautiful.

12. Lana's dog has a _____ sense of hearing.

13. Because Jorge wants all the books, I would say he is a _____ person.

14. Chip's behavior in class is _____ because he blurts out words and walks around the room when he shouldn't.

15. In my English class, we are studying _____ words which are no longer used.

16. One should be friendly, not _____, to one's neighbors.

17. Food from Tahiti is my favorite _____ food.

18. When Adam makes a _____ remark in class, Mr. Williams always nods in approval.

19. She came from a _____ family of the Old South tradition.

20. He speaks with _____, a trait we admire and trust.

A. counsel

B. enable

C. candor

D. gaunt

E. annual

F. dawn

G. caution

H. greedy

I. genteel

J. keen

K. era

L. exotic

M. aviator

N. erratic

O. dapper

P. archaic

Q. ancient

R. hostile

S. rhyme

T. canny

STOP

WORDS AND THEIR MEANINGS

ACTIVITY: For each question, you are to decide which of the four answers is the most similar in meaning to that of the word in **bold type** above it. Circle the correct answer.

1. **Elevate** your head to lessen the pain.
   A lower
   B straighten
   C restore
   D raise

2. The firemen **searched** the house quickly.
   A ransacked
   B left
   C looked around
   D entered

3. She keeps a **diary** in her bedroom.
   A dairy
   B daily record
   C bank
   D notebook

4. Rafael **criticizes** Fabio too much in class.
   A finds fault with
   B praises
   C admires
   D annoys

5. The SCA has only one **inactive** member.
   A aggressive
   B stubborn
   C eager
   D nonparticipating

6. The team was **clad** in green and white.
   A painted
   B tattooed
   C clothed
   D provided

7. Don't **accept** rides from any strangers.
   A decline
   B take
   C possess
   D accompany

8. His lengthy work was all **in vain**.
   A vane
   B acceptable
   C to no avail
   D internationally known

9. The **creditor** wanted the money Jim's dad owed him.
   A money lender
   B money borrower
   C wife
   D institution

10. The UN quickly **mobilized** the troops.
    A congratulated
    B sent to Mobile
    C put at rest
    D put into motion

STOP

CHAPTER THREE:

ENHANCING READING COMPREHENSION

Learning to understand what you read is one of the most important skills you will ever acquire. One way to enhance your reading comprehension is to create a "mini-movie" in your mind as you read. In this chapter, several activities are presented that will improve your reading comprehension.

ACTIVITY: Read the following poem, "Memories of a Higher Realm," by Jeremy Hinds, and answer the three questions.

MEMORIES OF A HIGHER REALM

Jeremy Hinds

Billowing sails on pillowy masts
White, rolling ships on high
   windy blasts.
Then twisting about and
   changing of form
Then darken and thunder, and
   threaten with storm.
Eclipsing the sun with downy
   white wing
Like snow-covered flocks which
   silently sing.

While lying on hillsides on
   crisp autumn days
Imagining figures they shift to
   portray.
Like storybook pictures of
   towers and bells
Passing the days with their
   fantastic tales.
The playful children of the pure
   azure sky,
I can only wonder as the clouds
   pass me by.

1. In the line "The playful children of the pure azure sky," what does the word **azure** mean?
   (a) evil   (b) stormy
   (c) blue   (d) gray

2. What does the title "Memories of a Higher Realm" suggest about the author's attitudes or feelings toward clouds?
   (a) wonder of ships
   (b) tranquility of autumn hillsides
   (c) childlike qualities of the sky
   (d) beauty and wonder of clouds

3. In the opening line, "Billowing sails on pillowy masts," a metaphor (a comparison between two things) is used to compare clouds and sails. Look at the second line and decide to what objects the clouds are being compared.
   (a) blasts   (b) ships
   (c) wind   (d) sea

STOP

ACTIVITY: Read the following passage and answer the questions that follow with the best answer.

The brain is the largest and most important part of a person's nervous system. The human brain is about 3½ pounds of gray and white gelatinlike substance. It weighs only one-fiftieth as much as the body, yet it uses one-fourth of the blood's oxygen. The brain is an information storage space and a how-to library. It knows how to put facts and ideas together as well as how to figure out problems.

The brain is also a drugstore that fills its prescriptions in split seconds. When you are hurt, for example, the brain sends out a chemical called "enkephalin," which is a pain-killer. When you encounter a potential danger, the brain sends a chemical called "norepinephrine" through your body which in turn starts another chemical called "adrenaline" flowing to warn you of danger.

The brain is a message center, too. It's like a big telephone exchange with messages coming in and out all the time. Each second the brain receives more than 100 million nerve messages from your body, and it knows what to do with them.

1. A metaphor is a comparison that does **not** use **like** or **as**. Which of the following is **not** a metaphor for the brain?
   a. message center
   b. drugstore
   c. gray and white substance
   d. how-to library

2. A simile is a comparison that uses **like** or **as**. Which of the following is used in a simile that compares the brain to something else?
   a. information storage space
   b. gelatinlike substance
   c. nervous system
   d. telephone exchange

3. Which of the following substances warns the body about danger?
   a. adrenaline
   b. norepinephrine
   c. enkephalin
   d. prescription

4. The author of this selection uses the fact that the brain uses one-fourth of the blood's oxygen to show:
   a. how important the brain is
   b. that the brain is good storage space
   c. how small the brain is
   d. that the brain knows how to put facts and ideas together

ACTIVITY: Read the following excerpt from ***Trails to Treasure***, by David Russell, Constance McCullough, and Doris Gates. On the next page, answer questions 1 through 5.

MOZART, THE WONDER BOY

It seemed like any other January day in the little town of Salzburg, Austria. Housewives hurried back and forth on their errands, just as usual. And everyone talked about the weather, just as usual. There were a few people, to be sure, who knew that a baby boy had arrived at the house of Leopold Mozart. But babies were not unusual. It was a good thing, they agreed, that this second child was a son, since there was already a five-year-old daughter, Nannerl. But that was as much interest as they cared to take.

Certainly not one of the good citizens of Salzburg, except possibly the boy's own parents, could have guessed that this baby boy would make the twenty-seventh day of January a date to remember wherever music is loved.

"I wonder if he will be a musician," said Leopold Mozart as he gazed down at his new son. Leopold played the violin in the archbishop's orchestra and it was important to him that his son should like music.

"I think he will," Little Nannerl told him. "I want to be one."

Nannerl's real name was Anna Maria, but few people ever called her that. Wolfgang was the new baby's name, but the family soon began calling him Wolferl.

Nannerl's words proved to be true. Almost from the cradle, little Wolferl showed a marked interest in music. When the members of the archbishop's orchestra came to practice their music with Leopold, the baby beat time with his little fists. He seemed happiest when the sound of violins and of the harpsichord filled the house.

When he was three years old, he stood one day beside the harpsichord while his sister practiced her new piece.

"Now let me play," he said when she had finished.

"You are much too little to play," Nannerl said.

Wolfgang paid no attention to her words. Climbing up beside her, he placed his small hands on the keyboard and played the piece more perfectly than she had done.

When this show of musical talent was reported to him, Leopold began to give his son lessons. Wolferl learned so easily that he astonished his father. One day when the friends had gathered to practice, the boy picked up a violin and played it perfectly, though he had never had a lesson on it.

Now Leopold was certain that his son was indeed unusually talented. He decided that Wolferl and Nannerl should give concerts together.

1. Leopold wanted his son to what?
    a. play in the Archbishop's orchestra
    b. play the violin
    c. like music
    d. play the harpsichord

2. Salzburg, Austria, is located where?
    a. Europe
    b. Africa
    c. South America
    d. Middle East

3. Wolferl seemed happiest when he heard what?
    a. children playing
    b. his father's violin
    c. Nannerl playing the piano
    d. the music of the orchestra

4. Which phrase below most closely describes "when he was three years old, . . . he played the piece more perfectly than she had done"?
    a. normally talented
    b. unusually talented
    c. occurs regularly
    d. frequently normal

5. "When the members of the archbishop's orchestra came to practice their music with Leopold, the baby beat time with his little fists." What does the expression "the baby beat time" suggest about Mozart, even at a very early age?
    a. He was a spoiled child from the beginning.
    b. His parents allowed him much freedom, even as a young child.
    c. He had an understanding and appreciation of music almost from the cradle.
    d. He had temper tantrums and fits of anger, even as a young child.

STOP

ACTIVITY: Read the following passage on water and answer the questions that follow.

From the time of ancient Greece to the middle of the eighteenth century, philosophers believed that there were only four elements: earth, fire, air, and water. However, in 1781 an English scientist by the name of Henry Cavendish found that water was obtained from the combustion (burning) of hydrogen. Eventually, other scientists determined that the water molecule consisted of two parts hydrogen to one part oxygen. Today, we write the formula for water as H_2O.

Water is one of the most dominant substances on the earth. It covers about three-fourths of the earth's surface and makes up a large part of most organic materials. For example, about seventy percent of the human body is comprised of water. Many foods, such as eggs, cucumbers, and watermelons are made predominantly of water.

Water that occurs naturally is never pure. It contains gases from the air and minerals from the ground where it has flowed. The purest water is distilled water, which can be prepared by boiling tap water and then condensing it.

Some of the physical properties of water are surprisingly interesting. Water melts at 0 degrees Celsius or 32 degrees Fahrenheit and boils at 100 degrees Celsius or 212 degrees Fahrenheit. Deep water is often blue because of suspended impurities. Also, ice, in thick layers, is blue. On the other hand, glacial streams tend to have a greenish color due to suspended calcium carbonate. Because of the impurities in water, it is a good conductor of electricity. As a result, one should not go swimming in bad weather, especially if there is lightning. Pure water is a poor conductor of electricity.

1. What percent of the human body is made up of water?
   (a) 70
   (b) 92
   (c) 93
   (d) 75

2. The purest form of water is found _____ ?
   (a) in nature
   (b) in air
   (c) by distilling
   (d) from rocks

3. The formula for water actually means what?
   (a) two parts hydrogen and one part oxygen
   (b) one part hydrogen and one part oxygen
   (c) one part hydrogen and two parts oxygen
   (d) two parts hydrogen and no parts oxygen

4. The blue color in water in thick layers is because of which one of the following reasons:
   (a) reflection from the sun
   (b) suspended impurities
   (c) suspended calcium carbonate
   (d) reflections from the clouds

STOP

ACTIVITY: Read the following passage from the play ***The Miracle Worker***, by William Gibson. The story is about Helen Keller and how she learned to overcome her disabilities. After reading the passage, answer questions 1 through 4 on the next page.

KELLER *(embarrassed)*.	Oh, Katie, we had a little talk, Miss Annie feels that if we indulge Helen in these—
AUNT EV.	But what's the child done?
ANNIE.	She's learned not to throw things on the floor and kick. It took us the best part of two weeks and—
AUNT EV.	But only a napkin, it's not as if it were breakable!
ANNIE.	And everything she's learned is? Mrs. Keller, I don't think we should tug-of-war for her; either give her to me or you keep her from kicking.
KATE.	What do you wish to do?
ANNIE.	Let me take her from the table.
AUNT EV.	Oh, let her stay, my goodness, she's only a child, she doesn't have to wear a napkin if she doesn't want to her first evening—
ANNIE *(level)*.	And ask outsiders not to interfere.
AUNT EV *(astonished)*.	Out—outsi—I'm the child's aunt!
KATE *(distressed)*.	Will once hurt so much, Miss Annie? I've made all Helen's favorite foods tonight. *(A pause)*.
KELLER *(gently)*.	It's a homecoming party, Miss Annie. *(ANNIE after a moment releases HELEN. But she cannot accept it; at her own chair she shakes her head and turns back, intent on KATE.)*
ANNIE.	She's testing you. You realize?
JAMES *(to ANNIE)*.	She's testing you.
KELLER.	Jimmie, be quiet. *(JAMES sits, tense.)* Now she's home, naturally she—
ANNIE.	And wants to see what will happen. At your hands. I said it was my main worry, is this what you promised me not half an hour ago?
KELLER *(reasonably)*.	But she's not kicking, now—
ANNIE.	And not learning not to. Mrs. Keller, teaching her is bound to be painful, to everyone. I know it hurts to watch, but she'll live up to just what you demand of her, and no more.
JAMES *(palely)*.	She's testing you.
KELLER *(testily)*.	Jimmie.
JAMES.	I have an opinion. I think I should—
KELLER.	No one's interested in hearing your opinion.
ANNIE.	I'm interested, of course she's testing me. Let me keep her to what she's learned and she'll go on learning from me. Take her out of my hands and it all comes apart.

GO ON ➜

QUESTIONS ON *THE MIRACLE WORKER*

1. When Annie wants to take Helen from the table, Aunt Ev
   _____ Helen's behavior by saying "She's only a child."
   - ⓐ discourages
   - ⓑ rationalizes
   - ⓒ rebukes
   - ⓓ ridicules

2. When Annie tells Mrs. Keller "I don't think we should play tug-of-war,"
   who is the person in the middle?
   - ⓐ Annie
   - ⓑ Mrs. Keller
   - ⓒ Helen
   - ⓓ Aunt Ev

3. What was Annie's main worry?
   - ⓐ Helen in her family surroundings again
   - ⓑ Aunt Ev's crude remarks
   - ⓒ Captain Keller's military ways
   - ⓓ Mrs. Keller's social activities

4. When Annie says, "Let me keep her to what she's learned and she'll go
   on learning from me," she does not mean which one of the following
   statements?
   - ⓐ Everyone is her teacher and she should obey everyone.
   - ⓑ If Helen throws down her napkin, I need to discipline her.
   - ⓒ If I am to teach Helen, then her family must allow me to do this.
   - ⓓ If we keep Helen on track, she will continue to do well.

STOP

ACTIVITY: Read the following journal entry by Julie Davis, and then answer the questions that follow on the next page.

VACATION AT MULBERRY POND

(JOURNAL: JUNE 20, 1995)

Colors of mostly orange and yellow begin to drift in the sky as a welcoming sunrise falls upon Mulberry in the warm morning that I arrive. Rays of gold dance on the pond, beckoning me to the water to soothe the summer heat. Hardly waiting for the car to come to a standstill, I immediately dash for the pond, with renewed memories of the summer before and what lay in store for me this summer.

Retreating to this secluded log cabin out in the middle of the tall, lonely pine tress surrounded by colorful, fragrant bushes and other shrubs has been our family tradition for years. The pond reaches out into the pine forest, giving life to the surrounding, tame wilderness. Used to friendly human life, animals and wildlife roam the area with the same kind of contentment that the pond seems to reflect. And the lush green grass around the pond willingly supports all kinds of lady bugs and butterflies.

Later in the morning, after napping to the sound of chirping crickets and bullfrogs, I take a stroll around the pond, reflecting on the serenity of Nature herself. Noticing a beaver building its home and hearing a wild crow make its "caw . . . caw" sound help me to lose myself as I keep wandering along, driven by forces that seem naturally to pull me further into the majestic forest.

Hours pass before I realize that I am really lost, but I'm not caring too much since I feel I'm in the presence of friends. Slanting downward, the sun is peeking through, creating a security for my friends and me. Once, I stop to gaze at a bobwhite and her covey of twelve babies, scurrying about, looking for worms and other insects. As I sit alone quietly, I hear other sounds in the distant woods, sounds of communication, sounds of happiness, sounds of daily life.

In the late afternoon, after feeling there were still so many more things to explore and yet so little time left in the day, I begin to walk with no direction or purpose. As dusk begins to fall, a whole new host of friends find curiosity in my aimless walking. I hear a pair of mourning doves singing to one another, telling of their shared love. Conscious of the millions of crickets singing their lovely good-byes, I slowly wind my path back around to an area near the pond and the cabin. Then, gradually, I make my way to the pondside, and as I look into the water I see another day that will last forever.

GO ON

QUESTIONS ON *"VACATION AT MULBERRY POND"*

1. With whom does the speaker in the journal entry go on her vacation?
   a. no one
   b. her grandparents
   c. her family
   d. her best friend

2. At the end of the journal entry, when the speaker writes " . . . and as I look into the water I see another day that will last forever," what is she probably referring to in " I see another day?"
   a. her reflection
   b. another good memory
   c. her tomorrow
   d. her past

3. With which animal did the speaker come in contact after she discovered she was lost?
   a. lady bug
   b. beaver
   c. wild crow
   d. bobwhite

4. What kind of mood does the speaker present in this entry?
   a. serene
   b. nostalgic
   c. sad
   d. angry

5. When the speaker realizes that she is lost, how does she react?
   a. she begins to get scared
   b. she yells for help
   c. she doesn't care too much
   d. she begins to run nonstop

6. Words like "begin," "dance," "supports," "pass," and "hear" indicate that this entry is written in which verb tense?
   a. future
   b. present
   c. past
   d. answer not given

7. The word **retreating** as used in the second paragraph means what?
   a. to get help
   b. to lie down
   c. to withdraw
   d. to move forward

STOP

ACTIVITY: Read the following question-and-answer passage from *Earth Book for Kids* by Linda Schwartz. Then answer the three questions that follow.

Q. What is *recycling*?

A. *Recycling* is processing and treating discarded materials so that they can be used again. Materials that are commonly recycled include aluminum, glass, and paper.

Q. What are the three ways recycling helps the environment?

A. When we recycle, we save space. Things that have been thrown away are kept and reused. Thus, fewer discards find their way to crowded city dumps and bulging landfills. Outdoor spaces can be left open instead of being filled to capacity with mountains of trash.

When we recycle, we save energy. Of course, some energy is needed for the recycling process—to melt aluminum, to crush glass, or to convert newsprint into clean paper that can be used again—but recycling requires less energy than making new products from raw materials.

When we recycle, we save natural resources. In the recycling process, old materials are made into new products so fewer raw materials are used. Also, some of the coal, natural gas, water, or wood that might have been used to produce energy for the manufacturing process is not needed.

1. Recycling does all but one of the following:
   a. saves space and resources
   b. fills dumpsters with mountains of trash
   c. treats discarded materials so that they can be used again
   d. allows items thrown away to be reused

2. Recycling helps the environment in three very important ways. All but one is appropriate.
   a. old materials are made into new products so that fewer natural resources are used
   b. newsprint cannot be converted into a reusable item
   c. by saving space, fewer discards find their way to city dumps
   d. energy is saved by producing new products from discarded items

3. Recycling can be defined as
   a. a process by which items are not saved or reused
   b. manufacturing new products from raw materials
   c. processing and treating discarded materials so that they can be used again
   d. a process of treating discarded materials so that they cannot be used again

READING COMPREHENSION

ACTIVITY: The following passage, *"A Rising Force,"* was written by Jeremy Hinds, a student at Arab High School. Listen carefully as you read this passage. Then answer the questions that follow.

The sun splashed down through the leaves and fell on her face as she lay sleeping on the forest floor. The morning air was cool and seemed to whisper, "Wake up, little one." She stretched and sat up, rubbing her brown, almond-shaped eyes. The stream nearby was bubbling over the stones, and a bird's song burst out from somewhere high in the trees. She rose to her feet and greeted the morning with a smile.

The serenity of the morning seemed a sweet dream compared to the violent storms of the night before. The medicine man had said the spirits were angry. The only lights in the sky were the bolts of lightning with their cold white flashes of luminescence. The wind howled like one thousand screaming souls, yet she seemed drawn to them.

She left her village behind, slipping unseen through the trees. The swaying boughs seemed to urge her on through the night. Rising up before her, a stony pinnacle reached upward through a clearing in the forest like an ancient tower now grown over with vegetation. Without thinking, she began to climb.

She perched on top of the rock, looking out just above the treetops. Though the wind still blew, it wasn't the raging sweep of a storm, but rather a refreshing night breeze. Here, above the world, the trees whispered comforting phrases into the wind, and the earth seemed to tell her the storm would never do her harm.

In time, she descended from the stone and began to wander through the forest. The storm had subsided, and the forest floor was carpeted with new-fallen leaves and cushion-like moss. The earth invited her to rest there, the breeze wrapped its comforting arms around her, and as she lay down, the rustling of the trees lulled her to sleep.

GO ON ➤

QUESTIONS ON *"A RISING FORCE"*

1. When the story opens, where is "little one" sleeping?
   - ⓐ near a tree
   - ⓑ beside a stream
   - ⓒ in her bed
   - ⓓ on the forest floor

2. All but one of the following sights and sounds are found in the story:
   - ⓐ bubbling of a stream
   - ⓑ wild cries of a lonely turkey
   - ⓒ bolts of lightning
   - ⓓ whispering phrases of trees

3. All but one of the following statements are false as she lies down to sleep:
   - ⓐ The breeze wrapped its comforting fingers around her.
   - ⓑ The trickling sounds of the stream calmed her.
   - ⓒ The rustling of the bushes lulled her to sleep.
   - ⓓ The earth invited her to rest.

4. Read the third paragraph carefully. Paying close attention to context clues, what do you think is the meaning of pinnacle?
   - ⓐ big stone
   - ⓑ ancient tower
   - ⓒ large clearing
   - ⓓ high peak

STOP

ACTIVITY: Read the following story, then answer the questions that follow.

You've heard the story of how the mean old wolf took advantage of the three little pigs and blew their houses down. One by one, he destroyed their houses made of straw, sticks, and mud. Even though Mother Sow had warned them about the danger of building their houses out of weak materials that the wolf could blow down, the young pigs were anxious to get out on their own and begin their own lives. They didn't have time to save money and buy expensive brick for their new homes. However, it hadn't taken them long to realize their mistakes. They had left home proudly, but soon they felt unsure and alone. Each one came back, asking Mother Sow if she would be willing to take them in until they could decide what to do next.

Once back home the three little pigs were more considerate of what their mother had to say, even though they sometimes complained and disagreed. Mother Sow suggested they plan to build their new houses out of brick or rock, not out of sticks, straw, and mud. They did not have enough money to afford brick, and rock was scarce in the area, so they decided to use the resources that were available to them. Mother Sow had heard about a certain culture where the pigs had actually made their own bricks out of dried mud. Since they always had plenty of mud, the three pigs decided they would make their own bricks, too.

It took many months to make all the bricks they would need. Day after day, the three pigs worked from dawn to dusk in the hot sun. They scarcely had time to do anything else. With their goal in mind, they made every brick with care and determination, anticipating the day when all the hard work would pay off. They were becoming responsible, and this time they knew that they would not fail.

1. After the wolf blew their houses down, the pigs decided to do what?
   a. rebuild
   b. return home
   c. look for the wolf
   d. look for mud

2. With what materials did the pigs build their new houses?
   a. straw and mud
   b. rock and mud
   c. expensive bricks
   d. bricks made of mud

3. Which one of the following might not be an important lesson the pigs learned?
   a. It is important to learn to work together.
   b. It is important to learn responsibility.
   c. It is not important to listen to your parents.
   d. It is important to work hard and be patient if one is to succeed in life.

STOP

ACTIVITY: The following passage in **World Tales: An Anthology of Multicultural Folk Literature**, by Anita Stern, is taken from a story of the Arabian Nights. This excerpt involves a fisherman whose life is in danger. Read carefully, then answer the questions that follow.

"Great king of the genies," called the monster, "I will never again disobey you!"

Hearing those words, the fisherman became brave and said, "Tell me why you were locked up in the vase."

The giant looked at the fisherman and said, "Speak to me more politely or I shall kill you."

"Why should you kill me?" asked the fisherman. "I have just freed you. Have you forgotten that?"

"No," answered the genie, "but that will not stop me from killing you. I am only going to do you one favor: you may choose the way you will die. I cannot treat you in any other way. If you want to know why, listen to my story.

"I fought against the king of the genies. To punish me, he shut me up in this copper vase and put his lead seal on it to keep me from coming out. Then he had the vase thrown into the sea. I made a vow that if anyone freed me before a hundred years had passed, I would make him rich even after his death. But nobody freed me. I made a vow that if anyone freed me in the second century, I would give him all the treasures in the world. But nobody freed me. In the third century, I promised to make him king, always to be near him, and grant him three wishes every day. But nobody freed me. At last, I grew angry at being kept in the vase so long and vowed that if anyone released me, I would kill him at once and would only allow him to choose the way he would die. So you may choose the way you will die."

The fisherman was very sad. "What an unlucky man I am for freeing you. Please do not kill me."

"I have told you," said the genie, "that is impossible. Quickly, choose how you will die."

The fisherman began to think of a way to trick the genie.

"I really cannot believe," said the fisherman, "that this vase can hold your feet and even your whole body. I cannot believe it unless you show me."

The genie began to change himself into smoke, which spread over the sea and the shore. Collecting itself together, the smoke began to go back into the vase until there was nothing left outside. Then a voice came from inside the vase. It said to the fisherman, "Well, unbelieving fisherman, here I am in the vase. Do you believe me now?"

Instead of answering, the fisherman quickly took the lead lid and shut the top of the vase.

GO ON

"Now, Genie, you will ask me to pardon you!" shouted the fisherman. "And I will choose how you die! But no, it is better if I throw you into the sea. And I will build a house on the shore to warn other fishermen who cast their nets here. And so they will know not to fish up an evil genie like you."

When he heard those words, the genie did everything he could to get out of the vase. But he could not because the lid was tightly shut.

Then he tried to get out with a clever trick.

"If you take off the lid, I will repay you," said the genie.

"No," answered the fisherman, and he threw the vase far out into the sea.

---

1. Why is the genie planning to kill the fisherman?
   - O a The fisherman was mean to the genie.
   - O b The genie made a vow to kill anyone who released him from the vase.
   - O c The genie made a vow to kill anyone who freed him within a hundred years.
   - O d The fisherman stole the vase from the genie.

2. Which one of the following is not a vow made by the genie after being locked in the vase?
   - O a He would make anyone rich who freed him within a hundred years.
   - O b He would give anyone treasures of the world if he were freed within two hundred years.
   - O c He would kill anyone who freed him, regardless if it were one hundred or three hundred years.
   - O d He would make anyone king and grant that person three wishes a day if he were freed within three hundred years.

3. The fisherman, realizing that the genie was going to kill him, began to think of a clever way to trick the genie. The fisherman asked the genie to:
   - O a show him that the genie's feet and whole body could actually fit inside the vase.
   - O b swim out fifty feet and back in five minutes.
   - O c let him call his wife before the genie killed him.
   - O d spend the rest of the day fishing before the genie killed him.

4. After the fisherman locks the genie in the vase and is about to throw him into the water, the genie tries once again to trick the fisherman. What does the genie say?
   - O a "I will give you one million dollars if you open the lid."
   - O b "I will make you king if you open the lid."
   - O c "I will give you treasures if you open the lid."
   - O d "I will repay you if you open the lid."

STOP

CHAPTER FOUR:

DEVELOPING SPELLING SKILLS

The purpose of this chapter is not to teach the process of spelling but rather to refine the student's ability to find misspelled words. Experience has shown that the spelling section of major achievement tests is geared toward the student choosing, from a series of words, the one word that is correctly spelled or, conversely, incorrectly spelled.

The exercises in this chapter have been carefully chosen to take the student step-by-step through the process of learning to proof for spelling errors with speed and accuracy. Please note that the worksheets in the final part of this chapter are based on formats the student will be exposed to on various standardized achievement tests. Feel free to use some or all of the formats as your situation requires.

ACTIVITY: Read the words in each exercise and look for a spelling mistake. In the answer rows, mark the circle by the word with a mistake. If you do not find a mistake, mark the answer **No Mistakes**.

1. O a. bowl
   O c. suit
   O c. thus
   O d. habbit
   O e. No Mistakes

2. O a. unit
   O b. author
   O c. locate
   O d. recall
   O e. No Mistakes

3. O a. guessed
   O b. adjusted
   O c. instal
   O d. museum
   O e. No Mistakes

4. O a. promising
   O b. consisting
   O c. arriving
   O d. proveing
   O e. No Mistakes

STOP

ACTIVITY: Many of the questions in this exercise contain spelling mistakes. Some do not have any mistakes at all. In the answer rows, mark the circle by the word that contains a mistake.

 TIP *In each group, look quickly for a word that looks wrong. If all of the words are spelled correctly, mark **No Mistakes**.*

A.
1. scary
2. frieght
3. beneath
4. No Mistakes

B.
1. populate
2. describe
3. minister
4. No Mistakes

C.
1. enormeous
2. bulletin
3. syllable
4. No Mistakes

D.
1. official
2. treasures
3. festivel
4. No Mistakes

E.
1. conserve
2. discontinue
3. governor
4. No Mistakes

F.
1. declare
2. asisst
3. cautious
4. No Mistakes

G.
1. disappear
2. murmur
3. allowance
4. No Mistakes

H.
1. pioneer
2. postscript
3. sincer
4. No Mistakes

I.
1. pronounce
2. cerculation
3. examination
4. No Mistakes

J.
1. specailise
2. practice
3. nonfiction
4. No Mistakes

GO ON

K.
1. suitcase
2. trimme
3. celebrate
4. No Mistakes

L.
1. slimmiest
2. microphone
3. principal
4. No Mistakes

M.
1. waterproof
2. thoroughly
3. arangement
4. No Mistakes

N.
1. semicircle
2. commandor
3. marvelous
4. No Mistakes

O.
1. triangle
2. thirteith
3. seventy
4. No Mistakes

P.
1. astronaut
2. automobil
3. gasoline
4. No Mistakes

Q.
1. hessitate
2. vanished
3. envelopes
4. No Mistakes

R.
1. beneath
2. audience
3. explane
4. No Mistakes

S.
1. argued
2. industry
3. wonderful
4. No Mistakes

T.
1. happines
2. shortage
3. fertilize
4. No Mistakes

U.
1. creativity
2. tardiness
3. cancell
4. No Mistakes

FINDING THE MISSPELLED WORD

ACTIVITY: Look at each group of words and find the misspelled word.
Fill in the circle that has the same letter as the misspelled word.
Then, write the word correctly on the line.

1. a. insterment c. invitation ⓐ ⓑ ⓒ ⓓ _____
    b. exercise   d. misplace

2. a. wisdom   c. business   ⓐ ⓑ ⓒ ⓓ _____
    b. memory   d. valueable

3. a. visitor   c. prehistoric ⓐ ⓑ ⓒ ⓓ _____
    b. squirrell   d. moisture

4. a. criticize   c. hunddred   ⓐ ⓑ ⓒ ⓓ _____
    b. transport   d. celebrate

5. a. neighbor   c. opinion   ⓐ ⓑ ⓒ ⓓ _____
    b. skatboard   d. lightning

6. a. employment c. generous   ⓐ ⓑ ⓒ ⓓ _____
    b. chocolate   d. infermation

7. a. balanket   c. festival   ⓐ ⓑ ⓒ ⓓ _____
    b. straight   d. ancient

8. a. furniture   c. rehearse   ⓐ ⓑ ⓒ ⓓ _____
    b. yoursellf   d. solution

9. a. cottage   c. parade   ⓐ ⓑ ⓒ ⓓ _____
    b. freedom   d. dedline

10. a. conclude   c. disshonest ⓐ ⓑ ⓒ ⓓ _____
    b. flatten   d. themselves

11. a. excelent   c. impatient   ⓐ ⓑ ⓒ ⓓ _____
    b. priceless   d. adjective

12. a. library   c. luggage   ⓐ ⓑ ⓒ ⓓ _____
    b. oxygen   d. musseum

13. a. similar   c. generus   ⓐ ⓑ ⓒ ⓓ _____
    b. language   d. childish

STOP

FINDING THE CORRECTLY SPELLED WORD.

ACTIVITY: Fill in the bubble for the word that is spelled correctly and best completes the sentence.

1. My aunt owns two art _____.
   - (A) studios
   - (B) studdioes
   - (C) studioes
   - (D) studdios

2. Mother _____ with our maid.
   - (A) aregued
   - (B) argueed
   - (C) argued
   - (D) arggued

3. We _____ our plan to the committee.
   - (A) subbmited
   - (B) submitted
   - (C) submited
   - (D) subbmitted

4. Roger _____ the ball and made a touchdown.
   - (A) interrcepted
   - (B) entercepted
   - (C) intercepted
   - (D) inturcepted

5. My parents celebrated their twelfth _____.
   - (A) aniversary
   - (B) anniversery
   - (C) anniversy
   - (D) anniversary

6. It is your _____ to tell the truth.
   - (A) oblegation
   - (B) obligation
   - (C) oblagation
   - (D) oblagition

7. The senator gave a _____ speech.
   - (A) persuasive
   - (B) pursuasive
   - (C) perswasive
   - (D) perswasive

8. Chris is the most _____ person I know.
   - (A) conciderate
   - (B) considurate
   - (C) considerate
   - (D) considerete

9. She purchases all of the _____ for the department store.
   - (A) merchendise
   - (B) murchandice
   - (C) mershendise
   - (D) merchandise

GO ON

10. The sun set _____ across the desert.
    - (A) majestically
    - (B) majesticaly
    - (C) majestikally
    - (D) magestically

11. Review the chapter _____ with The Thirteen Colonies.
    - (A) beggining
    - (B) beginning
    - (C) begining
    - (D) biginning

12. The lawyer produced the _____ at the hearing.
    - (A) documant
    - (B) dokument
    - (C) documint
    - (D) document

13. Have you studied for your final _____ ?
    - (A) exumineation
    - (B) examination
    - (C) examanation
    - (D) exameneation

14. Can you _____ the last two questions?
    - (A) elliminate
    - (B) eliminat
    - (C) eliminate
    - (D) elimminate

15. Mozart was a very _____ composer.
    - (A) famus
    - (B) fameous
    - (C) fammous
    - (D) famous

16. The horse _____ at the starting gate.
    - (A) hesitated
    - (B) hesatated
    - (C) hessitated
    - (D) hesetated

17. My older sister is _____ today.
    - (A) sevinteen
    - (B) seventen
    - (C) seventeen
    - (D) seventene

18. Our class meeting is scheduled in the _____.
    - (A) caffeteria
    - (B.) cafeteria
    - (C) cafetiria
    - (D) cafitiria

19. Harriett baked a _____ pound cake.
    - (A) delecious
    - (B) dilecious
    - (C) delicious
    - (D) delishus

STOP

ACTIVITY: Read the following phrases. Three of the underlined words are spelled correctly. Find the phrase containing an underlined word that is **not** spelled correctly.

1.
- ○ A eighty years old
- ○ B a foreign language
- ○ C his chosen proffession
- ○ D a special award

2.
- ○ A the exotic perfume
- ○ B exchange this shirt
- ○ C a delicious meal
- ○ D the other opponant

3.
- ○ A publish a poem
- ○ B asembled in the gym
- ○ C reconsidered the answer
- ○ D circulate the papers

4.
- ○ A shadow puppets
- ○ B the pairachute jumper
- ○ C grocery shopping
- ○ D the mountain climber

5.
- ○ A the roar of thundar
- ○ B adjusted the door
- ○ C unsuccessful game
- ○ D geography lesson

6.
- ○ A pronounce the word
- ○ B a great stereo system
- ○ C a very popular student
- ○ D the freequent shopper

7.
- ○ A looked drouwsy
- ○ B seemed nervous
- ○ C difficult question
- ○ D reached a decision

8.
- ○ A immediate surrender
- ○ B clever commedian
- ○ C launched the boat
- ○ D a sense of direction

9.
- ○ A nest in the chimmney
- ○ B his loyal teammates
- ○ C several easy quizzes
- ○ D develop the film

10.
- ○ A supported the charity
- ○ B opened the umbrella
- ○ C continnued to study
- ○ D the vacant lot

STOP

CHAPTER FIVE:

EXPLORING LANGUAGE MECHANICS

It is important to learn how to communicate in written language. Through proper mechanical usage, we can better understand and relate to each other. When we study and understand any language, expression in written form becomes easier. Therefore, we must learn and understand any language in its written form if we are to live and work together successfully.

The purpose of this chapter is to develop and improve mechanical skills. The exercises have been chosen with emphasis on punctuation and capitalization. Working through these exercises, you can improve your achievement scores as well as have a sense of pride and confidence in your ability to use language.

PUNCTUATION

ACTIVITY: Read the following sentences. Fill in the circle by the mark of punctuation that best completes the sentence. If no marks are needed, fill in the circle by the word **NONE**.

1. "I have been waiting all summer to see the movie, said Jan.

   ○ "   ○ .   ○ ?   ○ !   ○ NONE

2. He said, "What time is it"

   ○ .   ○ ,   ○ "   ○ ?   ○ NONE

3. Help! I don't understand how to do my algebra homework

   ○ ,   ○ !   ○ .   ○ "   ○ NONE

STOP

PUNCTUATION AND CAPITALIZATION

ACTIVITY: Read the following sentences and circle the letter next to the line that is **incorrect**. If no mistakes are found, circle the letter by **No Mistakes**.

1. A Kate and Andrew are going
   B to china for Christmas. They
   C are planning to return Jan. 7.
   D No Mistakes

2. A Doesnt Amaia want to return
   B to Spain after her year's
   C stay in the United States?
   D No Mistakes

3. A "Lee," said the teacher. You
   B are to be congratulated for
   C your award-winning essay."
   D No Mistakes

4. A Stephanie's mother was voted
   B Mother of the Year by the teachers
   C because she had worked so hard.
   D No Mistakes

5. A "Jeremy, are you planning to go
   B   to the play tonight?" asked Sue.
   C "I dont have a way to get there,"
      she said.
   D No Mistakes

6. A Amanda Shea and Jon are three
   B of my favorite friends. We do so
   C many activities together.
   D No Mistakes

ACTIVITY: Read the following sentences and choose the answer that **correctly** replaces the underlined part of each sentence. If the underlined part is correct, mark **No Mistakes**.

7. "Brax, are you going
   <u>to the game</u>
   A to the game?"
   B to the game."
   C to the game?
   D No Mistakes

8. "Tomorrow, we are going
   on a class <u>picnic</u>
   <u>said</u> Miss Wimberly.
   A picnic," said
   B picnic?" said
   C picnic." said
   D No Mistakes

9. Last summer we went
   <u>to Orlando Florida</u>.
   A to, Orlando Florida.
   B to Orlando, Florida.
   C to: Orlando, Florida.
   D No Mistakes

10. In history class we are
    studying <u>slavery and in</u>
    science we are learning
    about reproduction.
    A slavery, and in
    B slavery and, in
    C slavery; and in
    D No Mistakes

STOP

PUNCTUATION AND CAPITALIZATION

ACTIVITY: Read the following letter and identify the mistakes by circling the letter of the line on which the mistake occurs.

1. A   P.O. Box 6188
    B   Santa Barbara, CA 93160
    C   Sept. 11 1995
    D   No Mistakes

2. A   Payne's Books For Young Readers
    B   P.O. Box 2862
    C   Greensboro, NC 27425

    D   Dear Sir,

3. A   I am in the sixth grade and my class has
    B   read many books this year. One of my favorites
    C   is bridge to Terabethia. Do you have any study
    D   guides that you can send to my friend and me?

4. A   My teacher has asked my friend, and me
    B   to give a presentation on this book to the class
    C   since we enjoyed it so much. We are scared.
    D   No Mistakes

5. A   I will be so happy if you send me some
    B   information. Thank you.

    C   Sincerely

    D   Samantha Goldsmith

STOP

PUNCTUATION AND CAPITALIZATION

ACTIVITY: Read the following passage, paying close attention to the underlined segments on the numbered lines. From the lists that follow, choose the answer that correctly completes the sentences.

1.   The United States has many national <u>parks stretching</u> from the east coast to the west coast. In fact, there are

2.   almost 50 national <u>parks, not</u> including about 250 other types of historical monuments, all of which are under the protection of the National Park Service.

Our parks contain waterfalls, canyons, caves, lakes,

3.   mountains, glaciers, beautiful <u>trees; all</u> kinds of foliage, and a variety of animals. My favorite park is, of course,

4.   <u>Yellowstone National park.</u>

1. A parks. Stretching	3. A trees, all
B parks; stretching	B trees. All
C parks, stretching	C trees: all
D No Mistakes	D No Mistakes

2. A parks; not	4. A yellowstone national park.
B parks: not	B Yellowstone National Park.
C parks. Not	C Yellowstone national park.
D No Mistakes	D No Mistakes

STOP

PUNCTUATION AND CAPITALIZATION

ACTIVITY: Carefully read the following sentences. All but one sentence in each group are incorrect. Choose the **correct** sentence by filling in the circle next to it.

1. ○ A These are Ashleys soccer shoes.
   ○ B "I can't go", she said.
   ○ C She asked, "What is the assignment?"
   ○ D doesn't he know the correct answer?

2. ○ A These are my book's.
   ○ B Hamburgers fries and cokes are my favorite.
   ○ C "Furthermore, he said, "let's win."
   ○ D I was once in Portland, Maine.

3. ○ A I could go alone to the movie.
   ○ B Is this the right answer," Jim asked.
   ○ C If I could, I would go to peru.
   ○ D Who said, "What do you mean?

4. ○ A Wayne Louise and I are here already.
   ○ B Who's going to the game?
   ○ C This is the last time we're going
   ○ D Everyone sang, songs of joy and praise.

5. ○ A Did he say he wanted to go!
   ○ B This the dogs leash.
   ○ C Lee High School was the first school to score.
   ○ D My School is getting a new art building.

6. ○ A My cat alex is sick.
   ○ B My cat Alcx is sick.
   ○ C My cat Alex, is sick.
   ○ D My cat, Alex is sick.

7. ○ A Bill warned, "the dog has rabies."
   ○ B We began school before Labor day.
   ○ C On Christmas Day, we met at Grandmother's house.
   ○ D My grandmother is going to South america in September.

8. ○ A Lets go swimming at the city pool.
   ○ B My friend lives in Topeka Kansas.
   ○ C He said that, "the paper is easy to read."
   ○ D He said that the paper is easy to read.

STOP

ACTIVITY: Read the following letter. Look carefully at the numbered, underlined parts. Then, below the letter, circle the letter that shows the best capitalization and punctuation for each part.

12152 Amber Hill Trail
Moreno Valley, CA 92557

(1) <u>august 2 1995</u>

(2) <u>dear Katie</u>

    I had the most wonderful birthday party ever. My stepfather and mother took two of my best friends and me to Disneyland last week.

(3)   We <u>couldnt believe</u> our eyes—the park was not crowded. There was not even a wait for Splash Mountain. Cool! Mickey even met us for my birthday lunch.

    The best part of it all, I met a girl named Maria who lives almost
(4) in your neighborhood in <u>Colorado Springs when</u> I call you next week, I will give you her phone number so that you can call her. I think you would really like her.

(5)   <u>your friend</u>

Rachel

---

1. A   august 2, 1995
    B   August 2, 1995
    C   August 2 1995
    D   No Mistakes

2. A   Dear Katie,
    B   Dear Katie
    C   dear Katie,
    D   No Mistakes

3. A   could'nt believe
    B   couldnt' believe
    C   couldn't believe
    D   No Mistakes

4. A   Colorado springs, when
    B   Colorado Springs. When
    C   colorado springs: When
    D   No Mistakes

5. A   Your friend,
    B   Your Friend,
    C   Your Friend;
    D   No Mistakes

STOP

CHAPTER SIX:

IMPROVING LANGUAGE USAGE

We learn how to communicate better with one another by exploring and improving our language skills. We also learn to appreciate and understand people better through a more proper usage and expression of words.

The purpose of this chapter is to help you learn to express your ideas correctly and more effectively. The exercises have been carefully selected with emphasis on language usage and expression. Diligently working through these sample exercises will improve your language achievement scores and help you considerably in your self-expression.

RECOGNIZING STANDARD ENGLISH

ACTIVITY: Carefully read the following sentences. Fill in the circle beside the line which contains a mistake. If there are **no mistakes**, darken the appropriate circle.

1. A ○ Chad don't like his new
   B ○ bicycle. He says the seat
   C ○ is low and uncomfortable.
   D ○ No Mistakes

2. A ○ Look at Holly's new puppy.
   B ○ It has a brown nose and
   C ○ white fur, but it's tail is black.
   D ○ No Mistakes

3. A ○ The new teacher said that
   B ○ we could go to the school
   C ○ library. Now, Whose going?
   D ○ No Mistakes

4. A ○ It is about time for
   B ○ him and I to go to the
   C ○ park to feed the birds.
   D ○ No mistakes

   STOP

RECOGNIZING STANDARD ENGLISH

ACTIVITY: After you have read the following sentences, fill in the circle beside the line which contains a mistake of usage. If there are no mistakes, fill in the circle of the line that reads **No Mistakes**.

1 A ○ In the park last Sunday, the
   B ○ little children was performing
   C ○ an ethnic dance for everyone.
   D ○ No Mistakes

2 A ○ It was he in the grocery store
   B ○ last night when my grandfather
   C ○ and I stopped in to get milk.
   D ○ No Mistakes

3. A ○ Everyone said that Jan had
   B ○ Broke her arm playing softball.
   C ○ Do you know for sure?
   D ○ No Mistakes

4. A ○ Don't set in that chair, Ben.
   B ○ It is broken and I must replace
   C ○ one of the legs. Thank you.
   D ○ No Mistakes

5. A ○ They are shouting to the team
   B ○ captain for Benjamin to come
   C ○ in. But it ain't his turn to play.
   D ○ No Mistakes

6. A ○ The math page was tore out
   B ○ of my notebook. I must have
   C ○ done it accidentally.
   D ○ No Mistakes

7. A ○ My stepfather saw two deers
   B ○ last Thursday when he was
   C ○ driving past the Smith Farms.
   D ○ No Mistakes

8. A ○ Even though I try every
   B ○ summer, I am not never
   C ○ going to learn to water ski.
   D ○ No Mistakes

9. A ○ Skeet is practicing his
   B ○ favorite dives for the 1996
   C ○ Summer Olympics in Atlanta.
   D ○ No Mistakes

10. A ○ When Betty first met Matt,
    B ○ they didn't like each other.
    C ○ Now, they is great friends.
    D ○ No Mistakes

11. A ○ Kit had wrote his mother a
    B ○ letter from summer camp.
    C ○ He had so much fun.
    D ○ No Mistakes

12. A ○ I don't have no money to
    B ○ spend on Susie at the game.
    C ○ Will she be mad at me?
    D ○ No Mistakes

Dear Mom,
I'm having so much fun.
Send cookies, please. Thanks,
Your son

STOP

RECOGNIZING STANDARD ENGLISH

ACTIVITY: Read the letter below and answer the questions that follow. Look at each underlined word and decide if it is correct. If not, choose the correct word from the list below. If correct, circle **No Mistakes**.

September 19, 1995

Dear Bill and Mary,

It has been a long time since I (1) <u>hear</u> from you. Will you be going back (2) <u>too</u> Concord, Massachusetts this summer? (3) Me and Ellie (4) <u>won't</u> to join you. There (5) <u>is</u> many things we need to talk about.

I heard from Walt, but he (6) <u>don't</u> know if he can join us. Please (7) <u>let's</u> me hear from you soon so I can (8) <u>made</u> some preparations.

(9)　　<u>You're</u> friend,

Dee

---

1. <u>hear</u>
   - A here
   - B he're
   - C heard
   - D No Mistakes

2. <u>too</u>
   - A to
   - B twos
   - C two
   - D No Mistakes

3. <u>Me</u>
   - A Ellie and I
   - B Ellie and Me
   - C I and Ellie
   - D No Mistakes

4. <u>won't</u>
   - A wasn't
   - B want
   - C weren't
   - D No mistakes

5. <u>is</u>
   - A was
   - B had been
   - C are
   - D No Mistakes

6. <u>don't</u>
   - A doesn't
   - B will not
   - C isn't
   - D No Mistakes

7. <u>let's</u>
   - A lets
   - B let
   - C leave
   - D No Mistakes

8. <u>made</u>
   - A have made
   - B will make
   - C make
   - D No Mistakes

9. <u>you're</u>
   - A Yore
   - B Your
   - C You are
   - D No Mistakes

STOP

EXPRESSING AN IDEA

ACTIVITY: In the following sentences, circle the letter of the sentence that **best expresses the idea**.

1. A There are many students in Australia students there have summer vacation.
   B Students vacation in January. Summer vacation for students in Australia.
   C Students in Australia have summer vacation in January.
   D In Australia, students vacationing in summer in January.

2. A When you do your homework, sit in an upright position and turn it off.
   B When you do your homework, you sit in an upright position and turn the TV off.
   C When you do your homework, sit it in an upright position and turn the TV off.
   D When you do your homework, sit in an upright position and turn the TV off.

3. A A tornado is a violent, funnel-shaped wind. Because it moves in a narrow path with high speeds.
   B A tornado is a violent, funnel-shaped wind that moves in a narrow path with high speeds.
   C Because a tornado moves in a narrow path with high speeds. It is a violent, funnel-shaped wind.
   D A tornado moves in a narrow path with high speeds that is a violent, funnel-shaped wind.

USE OF WORDS

ACTIVITY: Read the following sentences. Look at the underlined words in each sentence and decide the **best way** to rewrite it.

4. When we arrived at the theater, the play <u>begun</u>.
   A had begun   B begin   C had begin   D No Change

5. You can pass to the seventh grade <u>before</u> you complete the sixth grade.
   A during   B meantime   C after   D No Change

6. After Jessie <u>had wrote</u> her poem, she <u>will read</u> it.
   A had written, will read   C had wrote, read
   B had written, read   D had written, had read

7. The class sat and watched as Kip <u>will read</u> his story.
   A has read   B will have read   C read   D No Change

8. Jennifer's idea <u>of walking</u> in the dark street was not a good one.
   A to walk   B having walked   C had walking   D No Change

STOP

RECOGNIZING STANDARD ENGLISH

ACTIVITY: Pay close attention to each numbered sentence and underlined word as you read the following paragraph. Answer the questions that follow by circling the correct letter.

---

(1) He is always glad to <u>helping</u> me. (2) Sometimes, he lets me help him gather the eggs from the chicken nests in the henhouse. (3) I have five cousins who live out of state. (4) He <u>don't</u> smoke a pipe now, but when he did, he would let me light it for him. (5) <u>Seeing that</u> I am the only grandchild that lives close to him, <u>him and me</u> get to do a lot of things together. (6) Last Saturday he and I <u>gone</u> down to the creek and walked around and talked.

---

1. Which sentence should be omitted from the paragraph?
   A. 1   B. 3   C. 4   D. 6

2. What is the **best** opening sentence for the paragraph?
   A. My grandfather and grandmother are great grandparents.
   B. My grandfather enjoys working on his farm.
   C. My grandfather and I are best friends.
   D. My grandfather does a lot of things with his grandchildren.

3. Read sentence 5 and decide the **best** way to rewrite the opening.
   A. Because   B. Also   C. When   D. After

4. Read sentence 5 and decide the **best** way to rewrite **"him and me."**
   A. he and me   B. me and him   C. me and he   D. he and I

5. Choose the **best** word for the underlined word in sentence 1.
   A. had helped   B. helped   C. help   D. have help

6. In sentence 6, choose the **best** word for the underlined word.
   A. went   B. had went   C. have gone   D. go

STOP

CHOOSING A SUBJECT

ACTIVITY: Read the following sentences and darken the circle underneath the subject.

1. Many <u>kangaroos</u> <u>are found</u> in the <u>Outback</u> in <u>Australia</u>.

    A ○   B ○   C ○   D ○

2. <u>Bunja's</u> <u>dad</u> is <u>considering</u> coming to our <u>school</u> to make a speech.

  A ○ B ○   C ○   D ○

3. <u>There</u> are six delicious <u>apples</u> in the <u>refrigerator</u> for <u>you</u>.

  A ○   B ○   C ○   D ○

4. The <u>countries</u> of <u>Southeast Asia</u> lie almost <u>entirely</u> in the <u>tropics</u>.

    A ○   B ○   C ○   D ○

5. <u>Delaware and Rhode Island</u> are the <u>smallest</u> <u>states</u> in the <u>United States</u>.

    A ○   B ○ C ○   D ○

CHOOSING A VERB

ACTIVITY: Read the following sentences and darken the circle underneath the verb (predicate).

6. <u>Here</u> <u>is</u> my little <u>brother</u> <u>who</u> is in the first grade.

  A ○ B ○   C ○ D ○

7. You <u>may go</u> to the <u>library</u> this <u>morning</u> to get a <u>book</u>.

    A ○   B ○   C ○   D ○

8. I <u>am running</u> for <u>president</u> of the <u>sixth</u> grade <u>class</u>.

    A ○   B ○   C ○   D ○

9. Mike <u>will create</u> a <u>large</u> display of his <u>paintings</u> this <u>afternoon</u>.

    A ○   B ○   C ○   D ○

10. The <u>fifth grade</u> boys <u>were talking</u> <u>during</u> the assembly <u>program</u>.

    A ○   B ○ C ○   D ○

STOP

COMBINING SENTENCES

ACTIVITY: Read the following sentences and choose the answer which is the best combination of the ideas presented.

1. Levente is a foreign exchange student. Levente is from Budapest, Hungary. Levente attends an American high school.
   A Levente is a foreign exchange student from Budapest, Hungary, and he attends an American high school.
   B Levente, a foreign exchange student, is from Budapest, Hungary, and Levente attends an American high school.
   C Levente, a foreign exchange student from Budapest, Hungary, attends an American high school.
   D Levente is a foreign exchange student and is from Budapest, Hungary, and attends an American high school.

2. Jeremiah went on a Mexican tour with me. Jeremiah is a college student.
   A Jeremiah went on a Mexican tour with me and now is a college student.
   B Jeremiah, a college student, went on a Mexican tour with me.
   C Jeremiah is a college student, and he went on a Mexican tour with me.
   D Even though Jeremiah is a college student, he went on a Mexican tour with me.

3. The library is closed today. The library is being repainted and recarpeted.
   A Being closed today, the library is being repainted and recarpeted.
   B Because the library is closed today, it is being repainted and recarpeted.
   C The library is closed today, and it is being repainted and recarpeted.
   D The library is being repainted and recarpeted today and it is closed.

STOP

CHOOSING A TOPIC SENTENCE

ACTIVITY: Carefully read the following paragraphs and decide which sentence would make the best topic sentence.

1. _____. They provide homes for many animals, including birds, squirrels, monkeys, raccoons, and certain types of insects. They also provide shade for certain types of foliage and for certain animals, including human beings. Also, they give off oxygen which is important for humans to live. Finally, and very importantly, they provide a sense of wonder and beauty to our landscape.
   A. They are important in our environment for many reasons.
   B. Trees are fun to climb.
   C. Trees are important in our environment for many reasons.
   D. Trees are necessary for everything to live.

2. _____. He started the Civil Rights Movement in the 1960's. He led many nonviolent marches and protests, trying to help the African-Americans obtain the rights they deserved. Often, Dr. King was mistreated and abused because he was a Black man. In fact, he spent days in a Birmingham jail. A Black church was bombed in Birmingham, killing four little Black girls. Martin Luther King, Jr., has certainly become an outstanding civil rights leader of the twentieth century.
   A. Martin Luther King, Jr., was a great man.
   B. He was a great man who campaigned for an end to discrimination and inequality.
   C. Martin Luther King, Jr., was an African-American man.
   D. Martin Luther King, Jr., was a great man who campaigned for an end to inequality and discrimination.

READING A PARAGRAPH

ACTIVITY: Read the following paragraph and decide which of the sentences best fits into the blank.

3. To write a well-written composition or essay, you must realize that writing is a process and that organization is very important. After you have chosen your topic, brainstorm on a sheet of paper, writing down everything that comes to your mind. _____. This doesn't have to be well written or too organized yet; this is just a beginning. After you have organized your thoughts on the outline, begin writing your rough draft. The last important step is revision or editing which leads to the neat or formal copy.
   A Then, organize your brainstorm.
   B. Then, make some type of outline.
   C. Then, begin writing your paper.
   D. Then, brainstorm on another sheet of paper.

STOP

READING THE PARAGRAPH

ACTIVITY: Read the following paragraphs and choose the numbered sentence that does **not** belong.

1. 1. The wind is blowing gently across the lawn and a squirrel is scampering here and there. 2. Fall is in the air and a few leaves are already changing their colors. 3. I cannot do one of the math problems my teacher assigned for the weekend. 4. Two or three birds are dipping down now and then for a quick worm or a drink of fresh water. 5. Another change of a season and I am lucky to be a part of it.

    A. Sentence 1   B. Sentence 3   C. Sentence 4   D. Sentence 5

2. 1. The night was filled with great excitement. 2. Everyone was there, hiding somewhere in the house, waiting in anticipation. 3. They had planned this surprise for days. 4. Billy's uncle had been to Europe two times on the Concorde. 5. Billy was coming home from the hospital and also today was his birthday. 6. What a great night this is going to be for everyone.

    A. Sentence 1   B. Sentence 2   C. Sentence 4   D. Sentence 5

SUPPORTING THE TOPIC SENTENCE

ACTIVITY: After reading the following topic sentence, choose one of the sentences that **best** supports or develops the topic sentence.

3. The open-air markets in Cairo, Egypt, are fun ways to get good bargains and meet some interesting people.

    A. The people who sell their goods at the markets expect the visitors to bargain against their prices. It is through the bargaining process that one can get to understand and appreciate the Egyptians.

    B. I bought a pair of sandals that I still wear occasionally. The man who sold them to me was difficult to understand.

    C. There are all kinds of goods set out on tables and draped across carts and lines. Some of the fabrics are brightly colored and not too expensive.

    D. I remember meeting an old woman and her grandchild. They were dressed in their Arabic attire, rich in color and shape.

STOP

CHOOSING THE CORRECT WORD OR PHRASE

ACTIVITY: Read the following sentences and from the choice of answers, choose the one that correctly completes the sentence.

1. John could paint the house _____ if he had more help.
   - [ ] A more quick
   - [ ] B more quickest
   - [ ] C more quickly
   - [ ] D most quick

2. The Johnsons _____ in the choir next Sunday.
   - [ ] A are singing
   - [ ] B is singing
   - [ ] C had been singing
   - [ ] D has sung

3. _____ are old friends, but we haven't seen each other in years.
   - [ ] A Me and her
   - [ ] B She and me
   - [ ] C I and she
   - [ ] D She and I

4. One of the animals _____ sick again.
   - [ ] A are
   - [ ] B is
   - [ ] C is being
   - [ ] D have been

5. The referee _____ with me on every move.
   - [ ] A were disagreeing
   - [ ] B disagree
   - [ ] C disagrees
   - [ ] D has disagreeing

6. On the table _____ three big red grapefruits.
   - [ ] A is
   - [ ] B are
   - [ ] C has
   - [ ] D was

7. Amaia is the _____ girl in Spain.
   - [ ] A more beautiful
   - [ ] B beautifulliest
   - [ ] C more beautifuller
   - [ ] D most beautiful

8. Jan and her brother _____ go to the park every day.
   - [ ] A don't
   - [ ] B doesn't
   - [ ] C don't never
   - [ ] D doesn't never

9. My father _____ my skateboard after I had fallen.
   - [ ] A repair
   - [ ] B repaired
   - [ ] C will repaired
   - [ ] D was repaired

10. Mrs. Moody _____ her students how to diagram a sentence.
   - [ ] A taughted
   - [ ] B teached
   - [ ] C teach
   - [ ] D taught

STOP

CHAPTER 7:

UTILIZING MATHEMATICAL CONCEPTS AND APPLICATIONS

Achievement tests always place special emphasis on how well students understand the number system and the terms and operations used in math. In recognition of this fact, Chapter 7 introduces the student to these skills in a typical test-taking situation.

The information in this chapter is presented in various formats so that the student will become more comfortable with the concept of test taking. Therefore, the authors have designed the activities in this chapter to provide the individual student with the tools necessary to be more successful on any future achievement tests. Working successfully through these exercises will improve the student's sense of pride and confidence in all areas of study.

MAKING USE OF MATHEMATICAL CONCEPTS

ACTIVITY: Read the following problems. There are four answers given for each question. You are to select the answer that you think is better than any of the others.

1. How many even numbers are there between 13 and 21?
   a. 3   b. 2   c. 4   d. 5

2. The closest estimate of $59.25 ÷ 6 is what?
   a. $9   b. $10   c. $8   d. $11

3. If N + 8 = 92, then N is what?
   a. 84   b. 11   c. 100   d. 85

STOP

PRACTICING ESTIMATION SKILLS

ACTIVITY: Read the following problems and fill in the circle of the best answer.

1. The closest estimate of 753 – 349 is between what?
   Ⓐ 450 and 500   Ⓒ 300 and 350
   Ⓑ 350 and 400   Ⓓ 400 and 450

2. If the cost of a can of tuna is $.59, and you buy 10 cans, what is the closest estimate of the total cost?
   Ⓐ $5.00   Ⓑ $6.00   Ⓒ $7.00   Ⓓ $8.00

3. The closest estimate of 422.72 – 149.22 is between what?
   Ⓐ 550 and 600   Ⓒ 250 and 300
   Ⓑ 400 and 450   Ⓓ 200 and 250

4. Look at the following circle. What is the closest estimate of the distance from A to C?
   Ⓐ 5″ and 5½″   Ⓒ 4½″ and 5″
   Ⓑ 5½″ and 6″   Ⓓ Not Given

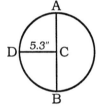

5. Which of the following shapes is a rectangle?

   Ⓐ   Ⓑ   Ⓒ   Ⓓ

6. Complete the following equation or inequality to create a true statement.

   $$\tfrac{5}{8} + \tfrac{1}{8} \underline{\quad ? \quad} 1$$

   Ⓐ =   Ⓑ >   Ⓒ <   Ⓓ Not Given

7. Of the following expressions, which one is the greatest in value?
   Ⓐ (8 x 2) + 7   Ⓑ (8 ÷ 2) + 7   Ⓒ (8 – 2) + 7   Ⓓ (8 + 2) + 7

8. If I had a ribbon that was 20 inches long and I cut it into strips of 4 inches, what part of the original length would each cut piece represent?
   Ⓐ ¼   Ⓑ ⅕   Ⓒ ⅙   Ⓓ ½

STOP

SOLVING PROBLEMS USING BASIC MATH CONCEPTS

ACTIVITY: Read the following problems and then fill in the circle of the best answer.

1. When you multiply these two numbers together, you get 32. But when you add these two numbers together, you get 12. What are the two numbers?

   Ⓐ 8 and 3   Ⓑ 4 and 7   Ⓒ 4 and 9   Ⓓ 8 and 4

2. If Rafael put 31 coconuts into boxes and each box can only hold 5 coconuts, how many full boxes did he have?

   Ⓐ 5   Ⓑ 6   Ⓒ 7   Ⓓ 26

3. What is the perimeter of the following rectangle?

   4 inches | 10 inches

   Ⓐ 40   Ⓑ 24   Ⓒ 14   Ⓓ 28

4. Look at the following fractions in the box. How many are greater than $\frac{4}{8}$?

   $\frac{3}{12}$, $\frac{9}{16}$, $\frac{2}{3}$, $\frac{7}{12}$, $\frac{5}{11}$, $\frac{3}{8}$, $\frac{5}{8}$

   Ⓐ 3   Ⓑ 5   Ⓒ 4   Ⓓ 6

5. What is another way to write 56?

   Ⓐ (8 x 6) + 8   Ⓑ (8 x 8) – 7   Ⓒ (9 x 2) x 3   Ⓓ Not Given

6. What part of the square is shaded?

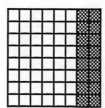

   Ⓐ $\frac{1}{5}$ Ⓑ $\frac{1}{4}$ Ⓒ $\frac{1}{3}$ Ⓓ $\frac{1}{6}$

7. The number ___?___ rounded to the nearest thousand is 45,000. The same number rounded to the nearest hundred is 45,400. What is the number?

   Ⓐ 45,339   Ⓑ 45,571   Ⓒ 45,328   Ⓓ 45,431

STOP

SOLVING PROBLEMS USING BASIC MATH CONCEPTS

ACTIVITY: Read the following problems and fill in the circle of the best answer.

1. The closest estimate of 31 x 40 is what?
   Ⓐ 1,300   Ⓑ 1,200   Ⓒ 130   Ⓓ 70

2. If gasoline costs $1.29 per gallon, what is the closest estimate of 10 gallons?
   Ⓐ $12.00   Ⓑ $11.00   Ⓒ $13.00   Ⓓ Not Given

3. The closest estimate of 2,321 + 2,873 is what?
   Ⓐ 6,000   Ⓑ 5,000   Ⓒ 7,000   Ⓓ Not Given

4. The closest estimate of $3\frac{3}{8} + 12\frac{4}{16}$ is what?
   Ⓐ 15   Ⓑ 14   Ⓒ 13   Ⓓ 16

5. Jorge rode his mountain bike 3 miles from his house to Adam's house. Then he rode 2 miles to get to the school. How many miles did he ride from his house to the school?
   Ⓐ 6   Ⓑ 5   Ⓒ 4   Ⓓ Not Given

6. If it takes Jason 1 hour and 30 minutes to drive to John's house and 1 hour and 25 minutes to drive to Cam's, how long does it take Jason to complete his trip?
   Ⓐ 2 hours 45 minutes
   Ⓑ 3 hours 10 minutes
   Ⓒ 2 hours 55 minutes
   Ⓓ 3 hours

7. Which of these figures forms a right angle?

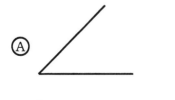

STOP

MAKING USE OF GRAPHING SKILLS

ACTIVITY: Carefully study the following graph. The graph shows the basketball scores in four games for the Knights and the Bulldogs. Answer the following questions.

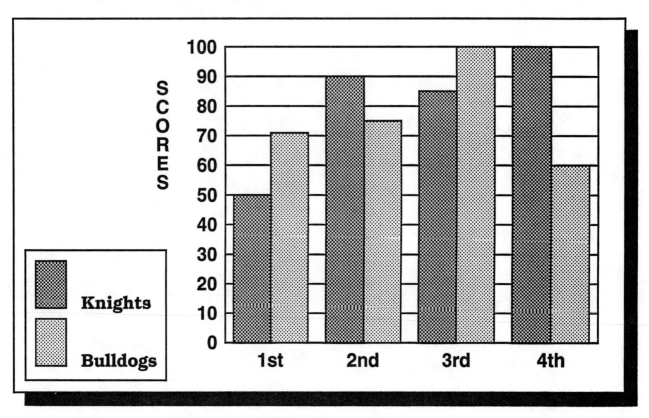

1. How many games did the Knights win?
   Ⓐ 3　　　　　Ⓑ 1　　　　　Ⓒ 2　　　　　Ⓓ Not Given

2. By approximately how many points did the Bulldogs beat the Knights in game 3?
   Ⓐ 15　　　　Ⓑ 20　　　　Ⓒ 5　　　　　Ⓓ Not Given

3. Which game had the greatest difference between the scores of the Knights and the Bulldogs?
   Ⓐ 1st　　　　Ⓑ 2nd　　　　Ⓒ 3rd　　　　Ⓓ 4th

4. What is the closest estimate of the number of points scored by the Knights in all games?
   Ⓐ 400　　　　Ⓑ 300　　　　Ⓒ 200　　　　Ⓓ Not Given

5. What is the closest estimate of the points scored by the Bulldogs in all games?
   Ⓐ 300　　　　Ⓑ 400　　　　Ⓒ 200　　　　Ⓓ Not Given

STOP

MAKING USE OF GRAPHING SKILLS

ACTIVITY: Study the following graph and then answer the four questions below by filling in the circle of the best answer.

CAR SALES FOR A LOCAL CAR DEALER

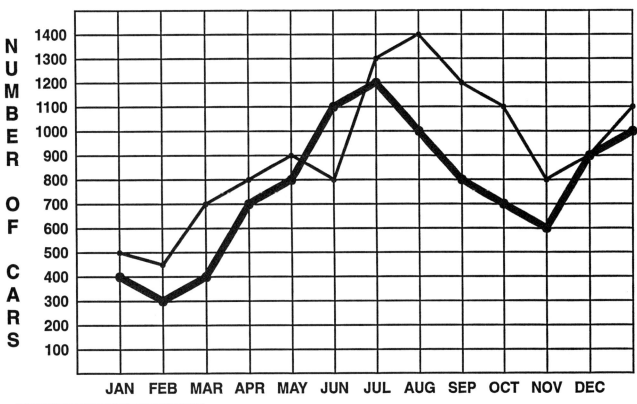

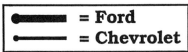

1. During which month did car sales reach their highest point?
   Ⓐ Jul   Ⓑ Aug   Ⓒ Sep   Ⓓ Jun

2. During which month did sales of both types of cars increase in volume?
   Ⓐ Jan   Ⓑ May   Ⓒ Sep   Ⓓ Nov

3. What is the closest estimate of the number of car sales for Ford during Jan., Feb., Mar., and Apr.?
   Ⓐ 1,900   Ⓑ 1,700   Ⓒ 1,800   Ⓓ Not Given

4. During which month did Chevrolet's sales slip lower than Ford's sales?
   Ⓐ May   Ⓑ Jan   Ⓒ Nov   Ⓓ Jun

STOP

SOLVING MATH WORD PROBLEMS

ACTIVITY: Read the following problems and then fill in the circle of the correct answer.

1. What is the written form for the number 35,060?
   - Ⓐ thirty-five hundred sixty
   - Ⓑ thirty-five thousand six hundred
   - Ⓒ thirty-five thousand sixty
   - Ⓓ thirty-five thousand six

2. Which number has a 3 in the hundredth's place?
   - Ⓐ 10.213
   - Ⓑ 100.132
   - Ⓒ 13.210
   - Ⓓ 12.310

3. Jeff has a rope 5 meters long. If one meter is approximately 39 inches, then approximately how many yards long is the rope?
   - Ⓐ 6
   - Ⓑ 5
   - Ⓒ 7
   - Ⓓ 4

4. Michael is having a party. He has to borrow 10 plates, 16 cups, 16 saucers, 6 forks, and 6 spoons. What fraction of the total supplies do the forks make up?
   - Ⓐ ¼
   - Ⓑ ⅛
   - Ⓒ ⅙
   - Ⓓ ⅑

5. There are three classes visiting the zoo. The first class has 23 students; the second class has 21 students; and the third class has 19 students. What is the average number of students in each class?
   - Ⓐ 24
   - Ⓑ 21
   - Ⓒ 22
   - Ⓓ 23

6. Which number below represents fifty and one half?
   - Ⓐ 50.125
   - Ⓑ 50.15
   - Ⓒ 50.5
   - Ⓓ Not Given

7. Which number represents 848 to the nearest hundred?
   - Ⓐ 800
   - Ⓑ 900
   - Ⓒ 850
   - Ⓓ 840

8. Which sign would make the following number expression true?

$$\tfrac{1}{3} + 2 \ \underline{\ ?\ } \ \tfrac{2}{3} + 2$$

   - Ⓐ >
   - Ⓑ =
   - Ⓒ +
   - Ⓓ <

STOP

MORE BASIC MATH APPLICATIONS

ACTIVITY: Read the following problems and then fill in the circle of the best answer.

1. Which number shows 742 represented to the nearest ten?
   Ⓐ 750 　　Ⓑ 740 　　Ⓒ 700 　　Ⓓ 800

2. Which number equation is not equivalent to 3 + 10 + 8?
   Ⓐ 8 + 5 + 8 　　Ⓑ 15 + 3 + 3 　　Ⓒ 3 x 3 x 2 　　Ⓓ 2 + 9 + 10

3. What is the missing number in the pattern?
   .08, 8/100, .37, 37/100, ___?___ , 24/100
   Ⓐ 2.40 　　Ⓑ .024 　　Ⓒ .25 　　Ⓓ .24

4. Study the following shaded Figure A. Then determine which one of the answers has the same fraction as the shaded area.

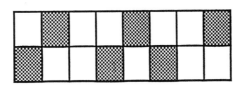

Figure A

Ⓐ
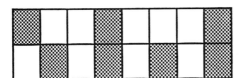

Ⓒ
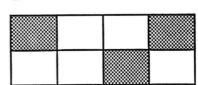

Ⓑ
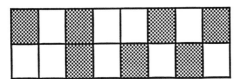

Ⓓ
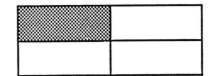

 　　 　　STOP

MORE BASIC MATH APPLICATIONS

ACTIVITY: Read the following problems and then fill in the circle of the best answer.

1. Anna is going to the humane society to choose a pet. She can have either a dog or a cat. There are three different breeds of dogs, and each breed is a different color. Also, there are two breeds of cats, and each breed is a different color. How many different choices does Anna have?

    Ⓐ 5   Ⓑ 10   Ⓒ 13   Ⓓ 11

2. Look at the number 76,359 and decide which of the following statements is true.
    Ⓐ It has a 3 in the hundred's place and a 6 in the ten thousand's place.
    Ⓑ It has a 7 in the ten thousand's place and a 5 in the hundred's place.
    Ⓒ It has a 9 in the ten's place and a 6 in the thousand's place.
    Ⓓ It has a 5 in the ten's place and a 6 in the thousand's place.

3. Which of the following measurements is the closest estimate of width of your hand?
    Ⓐ 1 meter
    Ⓑ 25 centimeters
    Ⓒ 3 inches
    Ⓓ 1 foot

4. Look at the word *television*. What fraction of the total number of letters in the word does the letter *e* comprise?

    Ⓐ $3/10$ Ⓑ $1/5$ Ⓒ $1/4$ Ⓓ $2/5$

5. Approximately what part of the following figure is the shaded area?

    Ⓐ .33   Ⓑ 2   Ⓒ .75   Ⓓ .67

6. Which of the following figures are congruent?

    Ⓐ   Ⓑ   Ⓒ   Ⓓ

STOP

MORE BASIC MATH APPLICATIONS

ACTIVITY: Read the following problems and then fill in the circle of the best answer.

1. In the following answers, what are the factors of 12?
   - Ⓐ 2, 4, 6 and 12
   - Ⓑ 6 and 12
   - Ⓒ 1, 2, 3, 4, 6, and 12
   - Ⓓ 1, 2, 3, 4, 5, 6, and 12

2. There are a total of 74 students in the fifth and sixth grades, but the fifth grade has 4 more students than the sixth grade. How many students are in each grade?
   - Ⓐ 40 in the fifth grade and 34 in the sixth grade
   - Ⓑ 39 in the fifth grade and 35 in the sixth grade
   - Ⓒ 40 in the fifth grade and 44 in the sixth grade
   - Ⓓ 38 in the fifth grade and 36 in the sixth grade

3. Which of the following units would most likely be used to measure the width of a football field?
   - Ⓐ kilometer
   - Ⓑ gallon
   - Ⓒ millimeter
   - Ⓓ meter

4. Look at the following chart. Then choose the estimate of the total number of students in all grades.

Students

Fourth Graders	125
Fifth Graders	160
Sixth Graders	223

   - Ⓐ 100 + 200 + 200
   - Ⓑ 100 + 100 + 200
   - Ⓒ 100 + 200 + 300
   - Ⓓ 200 + 200 + 200

5. Josh has 2 ten-dollar bills, 2 one-dollar bills, 3 dimes, 2 nickels, and 4 pennies. Caleigh wants to borrow $3.49 from Josh. How much will Josh have if he loans her the money?
   - Ⓐ $18.05
   - Ⓑ $18.90
   - Ⓒ $18.95
   - Ⓓ $25.93

STOP

CHAPTER 8:

IMPROVING MATH PROBLEM SOLVING AND INTERPRETATION

Recognizing and understanding the relationships that exist among numbers are important skills to know in our rapidly changing technological world. These skills are not difficult to learn; however, you must know them, especially if you are going to be using fractions, percentages, money, tables, and graphs.

The exercises presented in this chapter are developed to help you become a better student in such areas as addition, subtraction, multiplication, division, fractions, decimals, money, and problem solving. If you should have any difficulties with these exercises, don't hesitate to ask your teacher or parents for help. Furthermore, if you learn these skills now, your achievement scores will improve in mathematics and you will feel better about yourself.

WORKING MATHEMATICAL OPERATIONS

ACTIVITY: Read the following problems and then fill in the circle of the best answer.

1.
$$\begin{array}{r} 249 \\ + 278 \end{array}$$
Ⓐ 526
Ⓑ 527
Ⓒ 427
Ⓓ 528

3.
$$\begin{array}{r} 32.78 \\ - 28.24 \end{array}$$
Ⓐ 4.54
Ⓑ 61.02
Ⓒ 4.44
Ⓓ 4.64

2. $\frac{1}{7} + \frac{3}{7}$
Ⓐ $\frac{4}{7}$
Ⓑ $\frac{3}{7}$
Ⓒ $\frac{2}{7}$
Ⓓ Not Given

4.
$$\begin{array}{r} 14 \\ \times 6 \end{array}$$
Ⓐ 82
Ⓑ 72
Ⓒ 20
Ⓓ 84

STOP

WORKING NUMBER PROBLEMS

ACTIVITY: Read the following problems and then fill in the circle of the correct answer.

1.   32
      x 22
   Ⓐ 54
   Ⓑ 704
   Ⓒ 744
   Ⓓ 10

7.   794
      – 198
   Ⓐ 992
   Ⓑ 606
   Ⓒ 596
   Ⓓ 598

2. $6\overline{)5{,}320}$
   Ⓐ 88.666
   Ⓑ 8.86666
   Ⓒ 886.666
   Ⓓ 8,886.666

8. 6.9 – .54
   Ⓐ 6.36
   Ⓑ 7.44
   Ⓒ 6.30
   Ⓓ 6.44

3.   7.8
      – 0.54
   Ⓐ .26
   Ⓑ 6.26
   Ⓒ 8.34
   Ⓓ 7.26

9. $\frac{1}{4} + \frac{2}{3}$
   Ⓐ $\frac{3}{7}$
   Ⓑ $\frac{11}{12}$
   Ⓒ $\frac{3}{12}$
   Ⓓ $\frac{2}{7}$

4. 6 + .250
   Ⓐ 6.250
   Ⓑ 7.250
   Ⓒ 6.0250
   Ⓓ 5.750

10. 12.91 ÷ 3.01
   Ⓐ 428.0
   Ⓑ 42.8
   Ⓒ 4.38
   Ⓓ 4.28

5. $\frac{1}{3}$ x $\frac{3}{5}$
   Ⓐ $\frac{2}{15}$
   Ⓑ $\frac{1}{5}$
   Ⓒ $\frac{4}{15}$
   Ⓓ $\frac{2}{5}$

11. $\frac{1}{2}$ x $\frac{2}{6}$
   Ⓐ $\frac{3}{12}$
   Ⓑ $\frac{4}{12}$
   Ⓒ $\frac{1}{6}$
   Ⓓ $\frac{3}{6}$

6. $7\frac{3}{8}$
      $-3\frac{2}{16}$
   Ⓐ $3\frac{4}{16}$
   Ⓑ $4\frac{1}{16}$
   Ⓒ $4\frac{4}{8}$
   Ⓓ $4\frac{1}{4}$

12.   7200
      – 312
   Ⓐ 7,512
   Ⓑ 7,998
   Ⓒ 6,998
   Ⓓ 6,888

STOP

SOLVING WORD PROBLEMS

ACTIVITY: Read the following problems and then fill in the circle of the correct answer.

1. Desmond was given 10 problems for homework. André was given 8 problems, and Rafael was given 7. Calculate how many fewer problems Desmond had than André and Rafael had put together.
   Ⓐ 3   Ⓑ 1   Ⓒ 4   Ⓓ 5

2. Nathan went deer hunting with his dad. Nathan saw 6 deer early one morning. His father Dan saw 3 times that number late one evening. How many deer did Nathan's dad see?
   Ⓐ 9   Ⓑ 3   Ⓒ 18   Ⓓ 15

3. On her way to school Amaia stopped by Wendy's house, which was 4 blocks from school. Then she stopped at the grocery store, which was 2 blocks from school. How many blocks does Amaia live from school?
   Ⓐ 6   Ⓑ 8   Ⓒ Not enough information given   Ⓓ 10

4. If I feed my dog Jake 60 pounds of dog food every month, and 10 pounds cost $1.25, what is the cost of dog food per month?
   Ⓐ $6.00   Ⓑ $7.50   Ⓒ $48.00   Ⓓ Not Given

5. If Jake (see question #4) eats 60 pounds of food each month and 10 pounds cost $1.25, then how much will his dog food cost for one year?
   Ⓐ $90.00   Ⓑ $900.00   Ⓒ $480.00   Ⓓ Not Given

6. Mrs. McCoy collected $4.75 from each of her 27 sixth grade students for the Heart Association Fund. How much did she collect?
   Ⓐ $124.75   Ⓑ $128.25   Ⓒ $126.25   Ⓓ $128.75

7. Bianca left home at 7:45 A.M. After spending the day in school, she returned home at 4:15 P.M. How many hours and minutes was Bianca away from home?
   Ⓐ 7 hours, 30 minutes
   Ⓑ 7 hours, 45 minutes
   Ⓒ 8 hours, 15 minutes
   Ⓓ Not Given

STOP

SOLVING PROBLEMS USING GRAPHING SKILLS

ACTIVITY: Study the following graph and then answer the questions that follow.

BACK-TO-SCHOOL BOOK SALES AT SCHOOL STORE

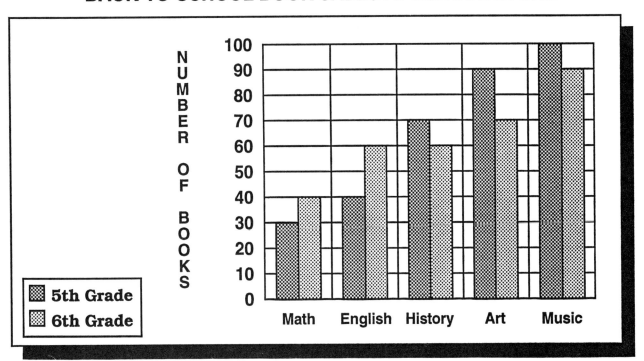

1. How many total fifth grade books were sold?
   Ⓐ 320   Ⓑ 430   Ⓒ 330   Ⓓ Not Given

2. How many art books were sold to the fifth and sixth graders?
   Ⓐ 160   Ⓑ 150   Ⓒ 170   Ⓓ Not Given

3. How many English and music books were sold to the sixth graders?
   Ⓐ 140   Ⓑ 150   Ⓒ 160   Ⓓ Not Given

4. If the back-to-school book sales were twice as much as last year's sales, how many books were sold last year?
   Ⓐ 1300   Ⓑ 350   Ⓒ 325   Ⓓ Not Given

5. How many history and math books were sold to the fifth and sixth graders?
   Ⓐ 190   Ⓑ 210   Ⓒ 230   Ⓓ Not Given

6. How many total sixth grade books were sold?
   Ⓐ 320   Ⓑ 330   Ⓒ 220   Ⓓ Not Given

STOP

WORKING BASIC MATHEMATICAL OPERATIONS

ACTIVITY: After each problem are three answers and an **"N"**
(meaning that the correct answer is **not given**). Work each problem
and compare your answer with the answers given. If your answer
matches any given answer, fill in the circle of the correct answer.
If not, fill in the circle around the **N**.

1.
```
   46
   76
 + 33
```
Ⓐ 165
Ⓑ 145
Ⓒ 155
Ⓓ N

7. 9 + (3 x 11)
Ⓐ 299
Ⓑ 42
Ⓒ 23
Ⓓ N

2
```
   31
   68
   29
 + 83
```
Ⓐ 201
Ⓑ 211
Ⓒ 221
Ⓓ N

8. 3.72 ÷ 24
Ⓐ 15.5
Ⓑ 1.55
Ⓒ 155
Ⓓ N

3.
```
    546
 x 4000
```
Ⓐ 221
Ⓑ 218,400
Ⓒ 2,184
Ⓓ N

9.
```
   4000
  x 600
```
Ⓐ 24,000,000
Ⓑ 240,000
Ⓒ 2,400,000
Ⓓ N

4.
```
    219
    356
    466
 + 385
```
Ⓐ 14,260
Ⓑ 142.6
Ⓒ 1,426
Ⓓ N

10. 12 x $\frac{6}{12}$
Ⓐ 7/12
Ⓑ 6
Ⓒ 12
Ⓓ N

5. 39 x 3212
Ⓐ 125,267
Ⓑ 125,269
Ⓒ 125,268
Ⓓ N

11. 68 – (4 x 6)
Ⓐ 44
Ⓑ 58
Ⓒ 78
Ⓓ N

6. $5\frac{2}{3} + 4\frac{1}{8}$
Ⓐ $9\frac{19}{24}$
Ⓑ $9\frac{13}{24}$
Ⓒ $1\frac{19}{24}$
Ⓓ N

12. 27 x 32
Ⓐ 59
Ⓑ 869
Ⓒ 864
Ⓓ N

STOP

USING A CHART TO SOLVE WORD PROBLEMS

ACTIVITY: Use the chart below to answer the questions that follow. Fill in the circle of the correct answer.

SCHOOL STORE	
SUPPLIES	**BOOKS**
Pencils .... 3 for 30¢	Math .... $ 9.95
Notebook .... $ 2.50	English 10.29
Pen 1.69	History 8.98
Marker 1.15	Art 7.69
Paper 1.98	Music 6.54

1. If Carl spent $2.40 for pencils, how many pencils did he buy?
   Ⓐ 18   Ⓑ 12   Ⓒ 24   Ⓓ Not Given

2. If Frank's mother gave him $30.00 to buy an English book, an art book, a pen, and 2 pencils, how much change did she get back?
   Ⓐ $11.13   Ⓑ $10.23   Ⓒ $10.13   Ⓓ Not Given

3. Lana's mother gave her enough money to buy the 5 books for sale at the school store. In fact, her mother expected change back from the money she had given Lana. What do we have to know to figure out how much change her mother will receive?
   Ⓐ How much the books cost.
   Ⓑ How much the books cost and how much money Lana's mother had given her.
   Ⓒ How much lunch will cost.
   Ⓓ How much the new ecology book costs.

4. Adam bought a music book and an art book. How much did he spend?
   Ⓐ $14.23   Ⓑ $13.23   Ⓒ $14.13   Ⓓ Not Given

5. If the store were to have a sale on the pens (2 for $3.00), how much would Trina save if she bought 2 at the sale price?
   Ⓐ 280   Ⓑ $1.38   Ⓒ 380   Ⓓ Not Given

MORE BASIC MATH OPERATIONS

ACTIVITY: After each problem are three answers and an "N" (meaning that the correct answer is not given). Work each problem and compare your answer with the answers given. If your answer matches any given answer, fill in the circle of the correct answer. If not, fill in the circle of the "N."

1. $313\overline{)919}$
   - (A) 29.9
   - (B) .29
   - (C) 2.9
   - (D) N

6. 78 x .06
   - (A) 46.8
   - (B) 468
   - (C) 4.68
   - (D) N

2. $427 \div 6$
   - (A) 71.16
   - (B) 71. 7
   - (C) 710. 1
   - (D) N

7. $\frac{5}{16} - \frac{1}{8} =$
   - (A) $\frac{3}{8}$
   - (B) $\frac{3}{16}$
   - (C) $\frac{4}{16}$
   - (D) N

3. $ 3\frac{6}{8}$
   $+ 6\frac{3}{4}$
   - (A) $9\frac{8}{16}$
   - (B) $10\frac{1}{2}$
   - (C) $9\frac{9}{16}$
   - (D) N

8. $ 50.3$
   $- 0.9$
   - (A) 49.4
   - (B) 51.2
   - (C) 49.3
   - (D) N

4. $0.781 + 0.289 =$
   - (A) .07
   - (B) 10.70
   - (C) 1.070
   - (D) N

9. $3.47 + 18 =$
   - (A) 21.53
   - (B) 22.47
   - (C) 21.47
   - (D) N

5. $ 891$
   $\underline{x\ 11}$
   - (A) 9,801
   - (B) 980
   - (C) 1,782
   - (D) N

10. $5 \times (320 - 285) =$
   - (A) 40
   - (B) 175
   - (C) 174
   - (D) N

STOP

SOLVING MATH WORD PROBLEMS

ACTIVITY: Read the following problems. At least three answers are given for each problem. You are to choose the answer that you think is better than any of the others.

1. Keith was one of the 20 sixth graders who won a prize. Prizes were also awarded to 25 fifth graders as well as to the fourth graders. Of the 55 students who won prizes, how many were fourth and fifth graders?
   - (A) 50
   - (B) 35
   - (C) 45
   - (D) Not Given

2. Chantz took 2 bags of chips and some drinks to the party. She had 6 times as many drinks as she had bags of chips. How many drinks did she take?
   - (A) 8
   - (B) 4
   - (C) 12
   - (D) Not Given

3. If Colleen has 9 pencils, 6 pens, and 4 markers, how can we determine how many more pencils she has than markers?
   - (A) subtract 4 from 9
   - (B) add 6 and 4 minus 9
   - (C) multiply 9 times 4
   - (D) Not Given

4. $4\overline{)603}$ =
   - (A) 1,507.50
   - (B) 15.75
   - (C) 150.75
   - (D) N

5. 7 + 0.89 =
   - (A) 70.89
   - (B) 7.89
   - (C) 71.89
   - (D) N

6. 6.4 + 0.68 =
   - (A) 7.08
   - (B) 6.08
   - (C) 6.98
   - (D) N

7. $6\overline{).03}$ =
   - (A) 5
   - (B) .05
   - (C) .005
   - (D) N

8. 3.3 x 0.13 =
   - (A) 4.29
   - (B) .429
   - (C) .0429
   - (D) N

9. 0.286 + 0.895 =
   - (A) .1181
   - (B) .1081
   - (C) 1.181
   - (D) N

STOP

CHAPTER 9:

INTERPRETING MAPS, CHARTS, AND DIAGRAMS

Learning to read maps, charts, and diagrams is an important everyday problem-solving skill. News reports, weather reports, current events, and travel, as well as many occupations, require the ability to read and to understand such illustrative tools. Gaining experience with maps, charts, and diagrams will help you develop the basic skills needed in school and in life. Work through the activities with your parents and teachers in order to improve your everyday problem-solving abilities.

LEARNING TO READ CHARTS

ACTIVITY: In a poll taken at Evansdale School, students were asked to indicate their favorite attractions for celebrating their birthdays.

FAVORITE ATTRACTIONS FOR CELEBRATING BIRTHDAYS

	SIX FLAGS	WHITE WATER	PLANET HOLLYWOOD	LAKE LANIER	PIZZERIA
4th grade	23	19	4	28	14
5th grade	29	13	11	18	20
6th grade	34	17	15	13	16
7th grade	37	11	24	20	12
8th grade	32	8	30	17	10

1. How many total students chose Six Flags over other attractions?
   - Ⓐ 145
   - Ⓑ 165
   - Ⓒ 155
   - Ⓓ 137

2. What attraction was the least favorite among all students?
   - Ⓐ Six Flags
   - Ⓑ Lake Lanier
   - Ⓒ Pizzeria
   - Ⓓ White Water

3. What two attractions were the most popular among fourth through eighth graders?
   - Ⓐ Six Flags and Lake Lanier
   - Ⓒ Six Flags and Planet Hollywood
   - Ⓑ Pizzeria and White Water
   - Ⓓ Lake Lanier and Pizzeria

4. What grade level had the most students polled?
   - Ⓐ 5th grade
   - Ⓑ 6th grade
   - Ⓒ 7th grade
   - Ⓓ 8th grade

STOP

LEARNING TO READ CHARTS

ACTIVITY: Henderson Mill School recently conducted a canned goods drive to help make Thanksgiving baskets for needy families. The chart below shows the total canned goods brought in by each grade level. Answer the questions below by circling the best answer.

GIVE A HELPING HAND

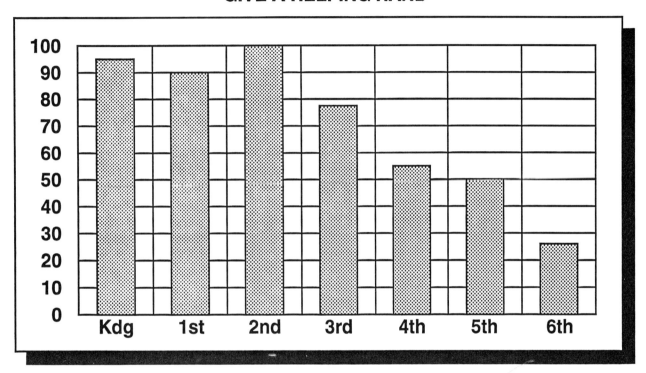

1. How many more canned goods did the second graders bring in compared with the first graders?

   Ⓐ 5　　　　Ⓑ 10　　　　Ⓒ 15　　　　Ⓓ 20

2. What was the total number of canned goods collected by the school on the drive?

   Ⓐ 399　　　Ⓑ 444　　　Ⓒ 469　　　Ⓓ 494

3. If 4 cans were placed in each basket, how many baskets could be prepared?

   Ⓐ 124　　　Ⓑ 120　　　Ⓒ 123　　　Ⓓ 103

4. Next year, if the school wants to collect 600 cans of goods, how many more cans must the students collect?

   Ⓐ 106　　　Ⓑ 114　　　Ⓒ 116　　　Ⓓ 294

5. How many total cans did the first through fourth graders bring in for the canned goods drive?

   Ⓐ 268　　　Ⓑ 324　　　Ⓒ 354　　　Ⓓ 304

STOP

LEARNING TO READ MAPS

ACTIVITY: Study the map of Washington, D.C., our nation's capital.
Then answer the eight questions that follow on the next page.

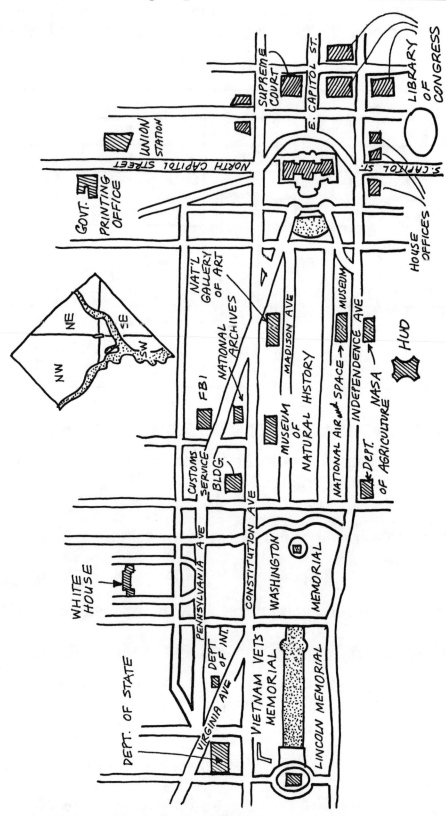

STOP

OUR NATION'S CAPITAL

1. The White House is located in what section of the map?
   Ⓐ NW   Ⓑ NE   Ⓒ SW   Ⓓ SE

2. Of the streets diagrammed, how many are named after former presidents?
   Ⓐ 5   Ⓑ 3   Ⓒ 2   Ⓓ 1

3. The Library of Congress is located on what well-known street?
   Ⓐ Pennsylvania Avenue   Ⓒ Virginia Avenue
   Ⓑ Constitution Avenue   Ⓓ Independence Avenue

4. The Museum of Natural History is located ____ (direction) of the FBI Building?
   Ⓐ NE   Ⓑ SE   Ⓒ SW   Ⓓ NW

5. What famous building is located at the center of five streets?
   Ⓐ Department of State   Ⓒ Washington Monument
   Ⓑ Capitol Building   Ⓓ National Gallery of Art

6. The National Air and Space Museum is located directly ____ (direction) of the National Gallery of Art?
   Ⓐ north   Ⓑ south   Ⓒ east   Ⓓ west

7. What area (NW, NE, SW, SE) in Washington, D.C., has the greatest number of buildings?
   Ⓐ NW   Ⓑ NE   Ⓒ SW   Ⓓ SE

8. At what site do we honor the men who fought in a particular war?
   Ⓐ The White House   Ⓒ Vietnam Veterans' Memorial
   Ⓑ Washington Monument   Ⓓ Lincoln Memorial

STOP

LEARNING TO READ MAPS

ACTIVITY: Use the map of Georgia to answer the questions below. Fill in the circle of the best answer.

1. How many miles would you travel from Dalton to Savannah if you used Interstates 75 and 16?
   - Ⓐ 358
   - Ⓒ 253
   - Ⓑ 254
   - Ⓓ 338

2. If you drove from Tifton to Augusta, which 2 directions would you travel?
   - Ⓐ north and east
   - Ⓑ south and west
   - Ⓒ north and south
   - Ⓓ north and west

3. On our family vacation last summer, we traveled from Atlanta to Augusta, then on to Waycross and finally to Valdosta. How many miles did our family travel?
   - Ⓐ 348
   - Ⓒ 409
   - Ⓑ 649
   - Ⓓ Not Given

4. If you drove from Bainbridge to Waycross, in which direction would you travel?
   - Ⓐ north
   - Ⓑ south
   - Ⓒ east
   - Ⓓ west

5. Matt's Delivery Service travels round-trip from Dalton to Valdosta three times each week. How many miles does Matt travel each week?
   - Ⓐ 325
   - Ⓑ 650
   - Ⓒ 1,300
   - Ⓓ 1,950

6. What cities are southwest of Macon?
   - Ⓐ Savannah and Waycross
   - Ⓒ Atlanta and Dalton
   - Ⓑ Columbus and Bainbridge
   - Ⓓ Columbus and Tifton

7. What cities are northwest of Macon?
   - Ⓐ Augusta and Savannah
   - Ⓒ Columbus and Tifton
   - Ⓑ Atlanta and Columbus
   - Ⓓ Atlanta and Dalton

LEARNING TO READ MAPS

ACTIVITY: Use the United States map to answer the questions that follow. Fill in the circle of the correct answer.

DO YOU KNOW YOUR STATES?

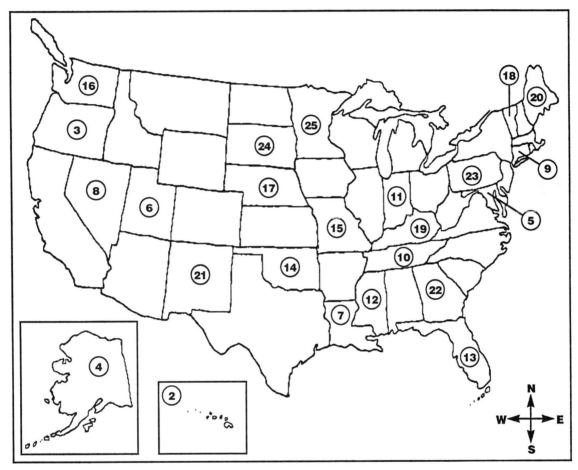

1. Tennessee, ⑩, is what direction from Georgia, ㉒?
   Ⓐ northeast   Ⓑ northwest   Ⓒ southwest   Ⓓ southeast

2. On the map, identify the state numbered ⑳.
   Ⓐ Maine   Ⓒ Massachusetts
   Ⓑ Pennsylvania   Ⓓ Florida

3. Identify the fiftieth state, ②.
   Ⓐ Hawaii   Ⓑ Alaska   Ⓒ Colorado   Ⓓ Wyoming

4. Which two states are West Coast states?
   Ⓐ ⑯ and ③   Ⓒ ⑳ and ⑨
   Ⓑ ③ and ⑧   Ⓓ ⑦ and ⑬

CHAPTER 10:

APPLYING LIBRARY AND STUDY SKILLS

It is important to learn to use the library because there are so many valuable resources available that can help you in almost any kind of research. In the library are found such resources as dictionaries, atlases, almanacs, encyclopedias, magazines, newspapers, and many more. Using these resource materials properly will make learning more fun and help save time when doing research on particular projects. Furthermore, if you feel more comfortable using the library, then you will become more confident as a student.

ACQUIRING LIBRARY SKILLS

ACTIVITY: Read the following questions and then fill in the circle of the correct answer.

1. If you were doing research on the first life forms on Earth, which book would be most helpful?
    Ⓐ atlas
    Ⓑ newspaper
    Ⓒ dictionary
    Ⓓ encyclopedia

2. If you were collecting information on the current presidential election, which source would probably be most helpful?
    Ⓐ dictionary
    Ⓑ magazine
    Ⓒ encyclopedia
    Ⓓ atlas

3. If you wanted to find out the meaning of the word *totalitarian*, you would probably use which source?
    Ⓐ encyclopedia
    Ⓑ atlas
    Ⓒ dictionary
    Ⓓ newspaper

4. If you wanted to find a map of the little island of Macau (located near Hong Kong), in which source would you look?
    Ⓐ magazine
    Ⓑ encyclopedia
    Ⓒ atlas
    Ⓓ dictionary

STOP

ACQUIRING LIBRARY SKILLS

ACTIVITY: Study the following computerized library catalog card. Then answer the questions that follow by filling in the circle of the best answer.

```
              MATERIAL:  Book
                AUTHOR:  Autexier, Philippe.
                 TITLE:  Beethoven: the composer as hero/Philippe A. Autexier.
           PUBLICATION:  New York: Harry N. Abrams, Inc., ©1992.
           DESCRIPTION:  143 p.: ill.
                SERIES:  Discoveries


               SUBJECT:  Beethoven, Ludwig van, 1770-1827.
   SERIES ADDED ENTRY:  Discoveries (New York, N.Y.)
```

1. How many pages does this book contain?
   Ⓐ 1,992   Ⓑ 143   Ⓒ 111   Ⓓ 1,770

2. When was this book published?
   Ⓐ 1770   Ⓑ 1827   Ⓒ 1992   Ⓓ Not Given

3. What is the name of the publishing company?
   Ⓐ Harry N. Abrams   Ⓒ Philippe A. Autexier
   Ⓑ Discoveries   Ⓓ New York

ACTIVITY· Read the following dictionary entry and answer the questions that follow by filling in the circle of the best answer.

school (skool) **n. 1** a place, usually a special building, for teaching and learning **2** the students and teachers of a school [an assembly for the whole school] **3** the time during which students are in classes [*School* starts in September.] **4** the full course of study in a school [They never finished *school*.] **5** any time or situation during which a person learns [the *school* of experience] **6** a certain part of a college or university [the law *school*] **7** a group of people who have the same ideas and opinions [a new *school* of writers] v. **1** to teach or train; educate [He is *schooled* in auto repair.] **2** to control; discipline [You can *school* yourself to be patient.] **adj.** of or for a school or schools [our *school* band] [This word developed from Old English *scol*, meaning "a place for teaching and learning," which was borrowed from Latin *schola*, having this same meaning.]

4. Choose the definition that portrays the word *school* as a verb.
   Ⓐ a place for teaching and learning
   Ⓑ to control or discipline
   Ⓒ of or for a school or schools
   Ⓓ time students are in classes

5. Which of the following definitions is reflected in this sentence: My friend Josh never finished school.
   Ⓐ2   Ⓑ7   Ⓒ4   Ⓓ1

6. From which language did the word school originate?
    ⒶFrench   ⒸGerman
   ⒷSpanish   ⒹOld English

STOP

ACQUIRING LIBRARY SKILLS

ACTIVITY: Look at the following title page and then answer the
questions that follow by filling in the circle of the correct answer.

Geraldine McCaughrean
One Thousand and One
Arabian
Nights
Illustrated by Stephen Lavis
Oxford University Press
Oxford   Toronto   Melbourne

1. Who wrote the book?
   - Ⓐ Stephen Lavis
   - Ⓑ Oxford Press
   - Ⓒ Geraldine McCaughrean
   - Ⓓ Jon Melbourne

2. In which city was the book published?
   - Ⓐ New York   Ⓒ San Francisco
   - Ⓑ Atlanta   Ⓓ Oxford

3. Who published the book?
   - Ⓐ University Press
   - Ⓑ Oxford University Press
   - Ⓒ Oxford Publishing
   - Ⓓ Melbourne Press

ACQUIRING LIBRARY SKILLS

ACTIVITY: Read the following chart of information on farming history
and then answer the questions that follow by filling in the circle of
the correct answer.

FARMING HISTORY

1900s: Chemicals as fertilizers and insecticides; plants that are disease-resistant; factory farming improves food production.

7000 B.C.: Discovery of how to grow grains; raise animals.

A.D. 600: Open-field farming system; sharing fields; crops in narrow strips.

1800s: New fertilizers, steam power, reaping and threshing machines; farming important in America and Australia.

4000 B.C.: Irrigating crops in Egypt.

1500s: New plants grow in America and Europe.

500 B.C.: Plows drawn by cattle; iron tools.

4. If you were asked to outline the above information in chronological
   order, with which line would you begin?
   - Ⓐ A.D.600   Ⓑ 4000 B.C.   Ⓒ 7000 B.C.   Ⓓ 1900s

5. If you were outlining the farming history in chronological order, which
   line would appear last?
   - Ⓐ 7000 B.C.   Ⓑ 1900s   Ⓒ 1800s   Ⓓ A.D. 600

STOP

ACQUIRING LIBRARY SKILLS

ACTIVITY: Read the following Table of Contents and then answer the questions by filling in the circle of the correct answer.

TABLE OF CONTENTS

---

1. Which story would mostly contain information about the Middle East?
   Ⓐ Chapter 10   Ⓑ Chapter 3   Ⓒ Chapter 5   Ⓓ Chapter 8

2. Which story would probably take place in South America?
   Ⓐ Chapter 9   Ⓑ Chapter 8   Ⓒ Chapter 2   Ⓓ Chapter 6

3. From which story would this sentence most likely come?
   The donkey tried every day to catch him as he passed through the cornfield.
   Ⓐ Chapter 4   Ⓑ Chapter 1   Ⓒ Chapter 5   Ⓓ Chapter 9

STOP

ACTIVITY: Study the following section from an index of a book. Fill in the circle of the best answer.

United States, information on the
Amusement parks, 523
Atlas, 34
Crime, 67
Currency, 9
Drugs and alcohol, 87
Education and schools, 356
Ethnic groups, 122
Foreign policy, 498
see also Wars
Geography, 287
Government, 137
see also State governments
Land area, 19
National parks, 340
Presidents, 25
Religions, 201
State capitals, 2
State governments, 150
Wars, 168
Washington, D.C., 43

1. On what page would you most likely begin to find information on former President Bush?
   Ⓐ 498 Ⓑ 137 Ⓒ 25 Ⓓ 43

2. Under which heading would you find information on Mexican-Americans?
   Ⓐ State governments Ⓒ Land area
   Ⓑ Ethnic groups Ⓓ Foreign policy

3. Which one of the following statements about the index is not true?
   Ⓐ It gives definitions of words and phrases.
   Ⓑ The topics under the U.S. are listed alphabetically.
   Ⓒ Information on government can be found in at least 2 places.
   Ⓓ Each topic is followed by a page number where the information can be found.

ACQUIRING LIBRARY SKILLS

ACTIVITY: Read the following library catalog card. Then answer the questions that follow by filling in the circle of the correct answer.

MATERIAL:	Book
AUTHOR:	Taylor, Mildred D.
TITLE:	Roll of Thunder, Hear My Cry / Mildred D. Taylor; frontispiece by Jerry Pinkney
PUBLICATION:	New York: Dial Press, ©1976.
DESCRIPTION:	276 p. : ill. ; 22 cm.
NOTES:	Sequel: Let the circle be broken. A black family living in the South during the 1930s is faced with prejudice and discrimination.

4. Who wrote the book?
   Ⓐ Dial Press
   Ⓑ Jerry Pinkney
   Ⓒ Mildred Taylor
   Ⓓ E. B. White

5. How many pages are in the book?
   Ⓐ 22 Ⓒ 276
   Ⓑ 1,976 Ⓓ 176

6. Who published the book?
   Ⓐ New York Press
   Ⓑ Mildred Taylor
   Ⓒ Dial Press
   Ⓓ Sequel, Inc.

7. Where was the book published?
   Ⓐ New York Ⓒ Los Angeles
   Ⓑ South Ⓓ Not Given

STOP

LEARNING TO READ MAPS

ACTIVITY: Study the following map of Arizona. Then answer the
questions that follow by filling in the circle of the best answer.

1. From Sedona, in what direction
   is the Grand Canyon located?
   - Ⓐ south
   - Ⓒ north
   - Ⓑ east
   - Ⓓ west

2. Which route would be quickest
   to get from Phoenix to Sedona?
   - Ⓐ 93
   - Ⓒ 60
   - Ⓑ 17
   - Ⓓ 69

3. To get from Globe to Tucson,
   which route would be the most
   direct?
   - Ⓐ south 80
   - Ⓒ west 76
   - Ⓑ north 77
   - Ⓓ south 77

4. What is the capital of Arizona?
   - Ⓐ Phoenix
   - Ⓒ Mesa
   - Ⓑ Glendale
   - Ⓓ Scottsdale

APPLYING RESEARCH SKILLS

ACTIVITY: Read the following
questions. Choose the best answer by filling in the circle.

5. Where would you find information on your home state?
   - Ⓐ magazine
   - Ⓑ encyclopedia
   - Ⓒ vertical file
   - Ⓓ atlas

6. If you wanted to find a map of Egypt, the country that King Tut ruled
   a long time ago, where would you look?
   - Ⓐ atlas
   - Ⓒ Reader's Guide to Periodical Literature
   - Ⓑ almanac
   - Ⓓ magazine

7. If you wanted to check out a novel written by E. B. White, where
   would you look first for a title?
   - Ⓐ encyclopedia
   - Ⓑ dictionary
   - Ⓒ magazine
   - Ⓓ card catalog

APPLYING RESEARCH SKILLS

ACTIVITY: Study the following dictionary entries and then answer the questions that follow by filling in the circle by the correct answer to each question.

art (art) n. 1. any specific skill that is not learned strictly by studying; the art of **writing** poetry and short stories. 2. creativeness. 3. works of beauty. 4. a making or doing of things to reflect or alter nature. 5. a branch of art, such as music or literature, etc. 6. a craft or its principles. 7. skill. 8. cunning. (Middle English, then French, then from Latin **ars**.)

1. What part of speech is the word **art**?
   - Ⓐ pronoun
   - Ⓒ noun
   - Ⓑ adjective
   - Ⓓ verb

2. The word **art** comes from what language?
   - Ⓐ Latin
   - Ⓒ Italian
   - Ⓑ German
   - Ⓓ Spanish

3. Which definition is employed in the following sentence?
   Jan has an **art** of expressing herself well in front of the class.
   - Ⓐ 1
   - Ⓒ 4
   - Ⓑ 6
   - Ⓓ 3

4. What part of speech is the word **Artemis?**
   - Ⓐ adjective
   - Ⓒ adverb
   - Ⓑ verb
   - Ⓓ noun

5. What is another name for Artemis?
   - Ⓐ goddess
   - Ⓒ Diana
   - Ⓑ Apollo
   - Ⓓ twin

Artemis (ar'- tə- mis) n. in Greek mythology, the goddess of hunting and the moon. Apollo's twin sister. Her Roman name is Diana.

artful (art-'fəl) adj. 1. clever or skillful. 2. exhibiting art. 3. imitative or artificial; not genuine. 4. crafty or tricky; cunning or deceitful. See **sly** for syn. n. art-ful-ness; adv. art'ful-ly.

6. What is the synonym for **artful**?
   - Ⓐ genuine
   - Ⓒ honest
   - Ⓑ sly
   - Ⓓ weak

7. What is the noun form of **artful**?
   - Ⓐ artfully
   - Ⓒ artfuller
   - Ⓑ artfulness
   - Ⓓ artfulliest

8. Which definition of artful is employed in the following sentence?
   The little boy was quite **artful** in the way he tricked his neighbor into thinking that nothing was wrong with the lawnmower.
   - Ⓐ 3
   - Ⓒ 2
   - Ⓑ 1
   - Ⓓ 4

STOP

ANSWER KEY

Page 15
1. competent
2. gossip
3. glowing
4. plan

Page 16
1. C
2. A
3. D
4. B
5. A
6. C
7. D
8. B
9. C
10. A

Page 17
11. D
12. A
13. C
14. C
15. A
16. D
17. B
18. C
19. B
20. A

Page 18
1. 2
2. 3
3. 4
4. 1
5. 2
6. 2
7. 1
8. 2
9. 3
10. 4

Page 19
1. horse
2. can't
3. their
4. too
5. I'll
6. feat
7. groan
8. paws, pause

9. It's
10. patients, patience
11. principals principles
12. seems, seams
13. week, weak
14. suite, sweet
15. weight, wait
16. fare, fair

Page 20
1. C
2. D
3. A
4. C
5. D

Page 21
1. D
2. A
3. C
4. B

Page 22
1. K
2. O
3. S
4. G
5. E
6. A
7. M
8. D
9. Q
10. B
11. F
12. J
13. H
14. N
15. P
16. R
17. L
18. T
19. I
20. C

Page 23
1. D
2. C
3. B
4. A

5. D
6. C
7. B
8. C
9. A
10. D

Page 24
1. C
2. D
3. B

Page 25
1. C
2. D
3. A
4. A

Page 27
1. C
2. A
3. D
4. B
5. C

Page 28
1. A
2. C
3. A
4. B

Page 30
1. B
2. C
3. A
4. A

Page 32
1. C
2. C
3. D
4. A
5. C
6. B
7. C

Page 33
1. B
2. B
3. C

Page 35
1. D
2. B
3. D
4. D

Page 36
1. B
2. D
3. C

Page 38
1. B
2. C
3. A
4. D

Page 39
1. D
2. E
3. C
4. D

Page 40
A. 2
B. 4
C. 1
D. 3
E. 4
F. 2
G. 4
H. 3
I. 2
J. 1

Page 41
K. 2
L. 1
M. 3
N. 2
O. 2
P. 2
Q. 1
R. 3
S. 4
T. 1
U. 3

Page 42
1. a. instrument
2. d. valuable
3. b. squirrel
4. c. hundred
5. b. skateboard
6. d. information
7. a. blanket
8. b. yourself
9. d. deadline
10. c. dishonest
11. a. excellent
12. d. museum
13. c. generous

Page 43
1. A
2. C
3. B
4. C
5. D
6. B
7. A
8. C
9. D

Page 44
10. A
11. B
12. D
13. B
14. C
15. D
16. A
17. C
18. B
19. C

Page 45
1. C
2. D
3. B
4. B
5. A
6. D
7. A
8. B
9. A
10. C

Page 46
1. "
2. ?
3. .

Page 47
1. B
2. A
3. A
4. D
5. C
6. A
7. A
8. A
9. B
10. A

Page 48
1. C
2. D
3. C
4. A
5. C

Page 49
1. C
2. D
3. A
4. B

Page 50
1. C
2. D
3. A
4. B
5. C
6. B
7. C
8. D

Page 51
1. B
2. A
3. C
4. B
5. A

Page 52
1. A
2. C
3. C
4. B

Page 53
1. B
2. D
3. B
4. A
5. C
6. A

7. A
8. B
9. D
10. C
11. A
12. A

Page 54
1. C
2. A
3. A
4. B
5. C
6. A
7. B
8. C
9. B

Page 55
1. C
2. D
3. B
4. A
5. C
6. B
7. C
8. D

Page 56
1. B
2. C
3. A
4. D
5. C
6. A

Page 57
1. A
2. B
3. B
4. A
5. A
6. B
7. A
8. A
9. A
10. B

Page 58
1. C
2. B
3. C

Page 59
1. C
2. D
3. B

Page 60
1. B
2. C
3. A

Page 61
1. C
2. A
3. D
4. B
5. C
6. B
7. D
8. A
9. B
10. D

Page 62
1. C
2. B
3. A

Page 63
1. D
2. B
3. C
4. A
5. D
6. C
7. A
8. B

Page 64
1. D
2. B
3. D
4. C
5. A
6. B
7. D

Page 65
1. B
2. C
3. B
4. D
5. B
6. C
7. B

Page 66
1. C
2. A
3. D
4. B
5. A

Page 67
1. A
2. D
3. C
4. A

Page 68
1. C
2. B
3. B
4. D
5. B
6. C
7. A
8. D

Page 69
1. B
2. C
3. D
4. C

Page 70
1. A
2. D
3. C
4. B
5. A
6. D

Page 71
1. C
2. B
3. D
4. A
5. C

Page 72
1. B
2. A
3. A
4. D

Page 73
1. B
2. C
3. D
4. A

5. B
6. D
7. C
8. A
9. B
10. D
11. C
12. D

Page 74
1. D
2. C
3. C
4. B
5. A
6. B
7. D

Page 75
1. C
2. A
3. B
4. C
5. D
6. A

Page 76
1. C
2. B
3. D
4. C
5. C
6. A
7. B
8. D
9. C
10. B
11. A
12. C

Page 77
1. C
2. C
3. B
4. A
5. D

Page 78
1. C
2. A
3. B
4. C
5. A
6. C
7. B

8. A
9. C
10. B

Page 79
1. B
2. C
3. A
4. C
5. B
6. A
7. C
8. B
9. C

Page 80
1. C
2. D
3. A
4. C

Page 81
1. B
2. D
3. C
4. A
5. B

Page 83
1. A
2. C
3. D
4. C
5. B
6. B
7. D
8. C

Page 84
1. D
2. A
3. B
4. C
5. D
6. B
7. D

Page 85
1. B
2. A
3. A
4. A

Page 86
1. D
2. B
3. C
4. C

Page 87
1. B
2. C
3. A
4. B
5. C
6. D

Page 88
1. C
2. D
3. B
4. C
5. B

Page 89
1. B
2. D
3. C

Page 90
1. C
2. B
3. A
4. C
5. C
6. C
7. A

Page 91
1. C
2. B
3. D
4. A
5. B
6. A
7. D

Page 92
1. C
2. A
3. A
4. D
5. C
6. B
7. B
8. D